The Servant Influencer

Harness the Power of Social Media for Positive Impact

By

Mikko Alasaarela

Copyright © 2023 by Heychain oy / Equel oy

All Rights Reserved.

It is not legal to reproduce, duplicate, or transmit any part of this document in either electronic means or printed format. Recording of this publication is strictly prohibited.

Dedication

To my wife Erja, who has been my unwavering support in my entrepreneurship journey and an amazing mother to our children. I am forever grateful to have you by my side.

And to my three incredible adult children, Aarni, Krister, and Inessa, who are my inspiration for making the world a better place. Your strength, creativity, caring nature, and empathy never fail to amaze me. Thank you for being my greatest accomplishment and source of pride.

Acknowledgment

This book was born from the Academy of Algorithmic Influence, a training program I developed over time to empower individuals to grow their online influence and make a positive impact. I am grateful to my colleagues at Equel - Filip Geppert, Jovana Djuricic, Ari Heljakka, Vadym Pasko, Christopher Shoo, Nikola Topalovic, Kristijan Trajceski, and Aarni Alasaarela - for their valuable input and participation during my Academy lectures.

A special thank you goes to Peter Scisco, whose invaluable assistance in writing this book was integral to its creation, and to Serena De Maio, who provided insightful feedback, creative ideas (including the title), and editorial support.

About the Author

Mikko Alasaarela, co-founder of Equel Social, is a sought-after expert in algorithmic influence and an international public speaker. He regularly advises companies, media houses, and government bodies on how social media influences people and how to use online influence for positive change.

Globally recognized impact entrepreneur, Mikko has leveraged his knowledge in algorithms to found and grow tech startups in San Francisco, Berlin, and Helsinki, positively impacting millions of people.

Table of Contents

Dedication	ii
Acknowledgment	iii
About the Author	iv
What Does It Mean to Be a Servant Influencer?	2
Preface	4
How My Journey Started	7
Independent Thinking	8
Emotional Intelligence	8
Why I Wrote This Book	10
1 An Introduction	13
We Live in the Age of Artificial Intelligence	13
How Algorithms Use Us	19
How Algorithms Tap into Our Consciousness	20
• How Algorithms Gain Our Attention	22
• How Algorithms Extract Behavioral Data	25
• How Algorithms Put Us to Work	26
• How Algorithms Trigger People to Pay	26
How Algorithms Shape Our Societies	28
• The Impact of Broadcast Media	29
• The Internet Years	30
• Social Media Changed Everything	30
• The Spread of Social Media Memes	32
What Went Wrong?	32
2 How to Make Friends and Gain Followers	36
Choose a Platform Based on Your Goals	37

Are You Building an Audience or a Community?	38
Which Networking Model Matches Your Purpose?	38
Friend Model	39
Follower Model	40
Interest-Based Model	40
Group Model	41
Algorithmic Model	43
Where Is Your Target Audience?	43
Should I Reveal My Identity?	44
Use Goals as Guides	45
The Entrepreneur	46
The Creator	49
The Advocate	51
The Educator	52
Growing Your Network	54
Making Friends on LinkedIn	54
Making Friends on Facebook	56
Gaining Followers on Twitter and Mastodon	57
Making Friends on Discord	59
Making Friends on Reddit	60
Making Friends on YouTube	61
• Create a Channel That's Specific but Not Worn Out	61
Making Friends on TikTok	63
3 How to Help People	**67**
Why You Should Help First	69
What Kind of Help Should You Give?	69

Participate in Conversations	70
Make Introductions	71
Share Positive Experiences	72
How to Help People on Different Platforms	72
LinkedIn	72
• Introduce People in Your Network	73
• Add Value with Thoughtful Comments	73
• Tag Relevant People to Help the Author of the Post	74
• Endorse People You Know	74
Twitter and Mastodon	75
Community Platforms (Discord, Slack, Telegram, WhatsApp)	77
4 How to Be Authentic and Stand Out	79
Profile	81
Give Your Professional Brand a Personal Touch	84
• Personal Character	84
• Professional Skills	85
• Talk Like a Human	86
• Find Your Communication Style	87
• Language Matters	88
5 How to Influence People	90
Earned vs. Manufactured Influence	92
Tactics for Winning Views	92
Who and When Matters	95
Special Moves You Can Make	96
Set Goals for Your Influence	98
Partisan or Bubble Bursting?	99

- Partisan — 99
- Bubble Bursting — 101

General or Niche Audience — 102
- General Audience — 102
- Niche Audience — 104

Shallow Impact on Many or Deep Impact on a Few? — 105
- Shallow Impact: Short-Term and Transactional — 106
- Deep Impact: Long-Term Commitment — 107

Leverage Your Platforms and Ride Waves — 108
- How to Draw Attention — 109
- How to Tell a Story That Resonates — 109
- How to Leverage Social Proof — 110
- How to Spark a Conversation — 111
- How to Ride a Wave — 111

Use Your Influence Superpower Responsibly — 111

6 From Influence to Opportunity — 114

Public vs. Private Conversations — 115

Virtual Conversation Guidelines — 118

What to Do and Not Do in Public Conversations — 119

What to Do and Not Do in Private Conversations — 120

Advancing Your Career through Influence — 122
- Greater Visibility Increases Remote Opportunities — 123

Grow Your Business with Influence — 124
- Grow Inbound — 125
- Improve Conversions with Social Proof — 126
- Turn Your Audience into a Community — 127

7 Building Communities   129

- Why a Community?   131
  - Communities Are Not Audiences   131
  - Don't Make Transactions, Guide Journeys   133
- From Mission to a Shared Cause   133
  - Ideal Community Members and What They Value   134
- Culture First, Growth Second   135
  - Superfans Spark Culture   135
  - Culture Sparks Subcultures   135
  - Culture VIPs   136
  - Keep Culture and Community Thriving   136
    - Notifications, Platforms, and Incentives   137
- Give First–It's the Only Way   138
- Guidelines to Keep It Together   139
- Winning Algorithm for Communities   140
  - Recruit Influencers to Reach Relevant Audiences   140
  - Build an Empathetic Culture that Cuts off Haters   141
  - Use Notification Flows to Keep People Engaged   141
  - Subcommunities Maintain Intimacy–So Let Them   141

8 Make a Positive Impact that Lasts   143

- Be the Change You Want To See in the World   143
  - Healthy Purpose   144
  - Advocate Healthy Behavior and Goals   145
  - Don't Manipulate People to Act against Their Own Good   146
- Break Bubbles to Open Your Mind   147
  - Build Trust with People Outside Your Bubble   148

Communicate in Their Language	148
Put Yourself in Other People's Position	149
Be a Servant Influencer	150
9 A Purposeful Life	152

I wrote this book for professionals who want to become servant influencers. If you want to become a thought leader or a community builder with a purpose, this book is for you. However, if you want to become famous, influence people anonymously, or spread disinformation, this book is not for you.

What Does It Mean to Be a Servant Influencer?

1. You Are Self-Aware.

Influencers driven by vanity and fame are often ignorant of their flaws. Servant Influencers, in contrast, are mindful of themselves. They know their qualities, weaknesses, values, sentiments, and emotions. In order to promote healthier and more fruitful conversations, the Servant Influencer must be self-aware and recognize their prejudices and shortcomings.

2. You Are Empathetic.

A Servant Influencer is able to identify and comprehend the thoughts, sentiments, and emotions that their message triggers in their audience. Such an influencer will be compassionate and able to connect with others. They are motivated by a sincere desire to assist and seek to understand other points of view.

3. You Are Committed To The Growth of Others.

A Servant Influencer's goal is to support and develop others. They tirelessly share their expertise and learn from those with different worldviews. They know that learning from and educating one another enables humanity to progress.

4. You Can Persuade.

Through their ability to persuade, Servant Influencers can affect other people's thoughts and behaviors. This is a valuable trait for turning influence into a positive impact. Servant Influencers only employ their power to positively influence others because they are dedicated to the wellbeing of others.

5. You Can Build A Community.

A Servant Influencer has the power to unite individuals around a shared objective. They promote a community spirit and give people a sense of belonging to something greater than themselves. Servant Influencers have a strong sense of responsibility for the communities they build and the causes they support.

Types of Servant Influencers:

- You are an entrepreneur on a mission.
- You are a creator and want to make a difference.
- You want to advocate a cause that you deeply care about.

You want to learn and educate people.

Preface

It was the autumn of 2019. I had recently returned to my native Finland from Berlin, Germany when I received a curious call from a screenwriter at YLE, the Finnish national public broadcasting company.

I had recently hosted a workshop for the social media team leads at YLE. The participants were worried about the negative effect of social media algorithms on their mission to deliver unbiased reporting to the population of Finland. An ever-growing portion of the news audience was discussing news on social media. Due to social media companies' desire to keep their users on their platforms, more and more people were participating in the news conversation without reading the original article.

This caused people in different filter bubbles[1] to see the same news in a different light, depending on the take their preferred influencer had on the news. This had become a direct threat to the ability of YLE to fulfill its mission. The initially neutral reporting could turn into multiple differently biased versions, depending on who was sharing the news.

The caller was Helena Lappeteläinen, a broadcast journalist who worked on screenwriting a popular TV show at YLE, focusing on current affairs. She said Finns needed to understand how easy it is for competent professionals to manipulate on a massive scale, even whole populations. To prove that, she asked me if I could manipulate

---

[1] Filter bubble is a situation in which an internet user encounters only information and opinions that conform to and reinforce their own beliefs, caused by algorithms that personalize an individual's online experience.

a large portion of Finns on social media and if I would accept to be recorded live for a short documentary that she would broadcast on her show.

I knew I could do that, but I hesitated. While I saw an opportunity to educate people, I worried they would hate me once they learned I manipulated them to give them a lesson. I answered that I would think about it.

I soon realized this was an opportunity to make an impact through influence. I would choose an important topic, which would benefit the population at large, and then disclose how I had manipulated social media to exercise that influence for educational purposes. It would be a double win.

The topic I chose was a deeply personal one. I was bullied in school from the early years all the way to university—often violently. It had a major impact on who I was, and it took me years to recover from the trauma and character flaws the bullying had caused. I had promised myself that I would never let it happen to my children.

I called Helena and agreed to take part in her documentary project. I said I wanted to influence the Finns to talk about school bullying because it was an important cause to me, and I believed it would benefit the population. Because the cause was good, I also believed Finns would forgive me for the manipulation.

I went to the drawing board and drafted a conversation opener that included narratives, timing, language, and content formats to make it viral. I also targeted specific people and groups to create a chain reaction through multiple filter bubbles for maximum spread. In essence, I was programming the readers' minds to react to my content in ways that enabled it to spread to everyone.

On the morning of Nov 12th, 2019, I met with the YLE production team. I had prepared well the day before and was relatively confident we would succeed. My story was in great shape, and I had done multiple similar influencing projects in English. But I still felt a bit nervous, as I had never done it on such a scale in the Finnish language, and I was under the watchful eye of TV cameras.

As the clock approached 9 am, I was ready to share my social media posts on Twitter, Facebook, and LinkedIn. The cameras went on. After a few words with the host, I pressed send.

As soon as the posts hit the feeds, my phone started ringing, and my message channels flooded over. TV cameras followed the action on my screen. After a few intense minutes, we knew we had succeeded. The speed at which the story was spreading across the country and social media platforms was incredible. Dozens of school teachers messaged me, and many local celebrities talked about it on their channels. Even my mom and dad called me, unaware of the discussion being part of a documentary project with YLE.

My posts received the direct attention of 650,000 Finns, and the conversation reached an estimated 2 million Finns in a country of 5.6 million inhabitants. I had persuaded a significant portion of the Finnish population to speak about school bullying.

Shortly after, the YLE stories came out on TV and their online news portal. People learned that I had deliberately made them all talk about school bullying for a documentary project, creating shockwaves across the country.

How My Journey Started

Have you ever thought about how much you have changed as a person over the years? I have—a lot.

Like almost everyone, I was a very different person at 20 than at 30 and different again by 40. During all those changes, I was lucky to gain an open mind and a strong will to expand my worldview, beginning as a young adult. Over the years, I have changed more than I could have imagined.

If you had known me during my late teens and early twenties, you would have known me as an outspoken, blunt, and bold person who talked loudly, interrupted everyone, and upset many people. I was ambitious and strong-willed, and my thinking was black-and-white. My character then resulted from years of bullying and isolation.

I was determined to show every bully that I was better than them. And so, despite the bullying and what I saw as my many faults and shortcomings, I did one thing right in my late teens. I set my life goals that I have followed over the years. My first goal was to become an entrepreneur and build ten companies during my lifetime. I am now running my eighth startup. I wanted to have a happy marriage with kids. I've enjoyed 24 years of happy marriage with my wife, and I can rejoice in three awesome adult children.

As welcome and life-affirming as those goals are, the most profound goal, the one that changed me completely, was to *become wise*. In my case, that amounted to three things: developing independent thinking and rationality, becoming knowledgeable and skilled in emotional intelligence, and designing and living out, to the best of my ability, a life of purpose.

Independent Thinking

My goal of becoming wise required me to commit to lifelong learning. I have spent countless evenings studying all kinds of topics that I found interesting. The books I've read include memoirs of past leaders, examinations of cultural evolution, and the history of religions. They encompass deep dives into behavioral sciences, emotional intelligence, and studies in economics like Levitt and Dubner's *Freakonomics*[2]. They also cover natural sciences, including topics such as Kaku's the *Physics of the Impossible*[3], conspiracy theories of all sorts, artificial intelligence and singularity, and many, many others.

Over the years, my worldview changed dramatically. Many things that I thought were facts turned out to be "alternative facts"—subjective beliefs that fit comfortably into my worldview.

Instead of comforting lies, I sought unpleasant truths. Over time, many of my firm beliefs came crashing down. The world turns out to be a complex and chaotic place where the truth is often unexpected, strange, and uncomfortable. During this learning process, which continues into the present day, I have tried my best to keep an open mind so that I can make further adjustments.

Emotional Intelligence

Wisdom requires more than a superficial knowledge of various disciplines. You also need to build skills in various areas of intelligence, most importantly in an area that Daniel Goleman popularized as *emotional intelligence*[4]. I define emotional

---

[2] Levitt, Steven D., and Stephen J. Dubner. 2020. *Freakonomics Revised and Expanded Edition*. New York: William Morrow.

[3] Kaku, Michio. 2008. *Physics of the Impossible: A Scientific Exploration into the World of Phasers, Force Fields, Teleportation, and Time Travel*. New York: Doubleday.

[4] Goleman, Daniel. 2005. *Emotional Intelligence: Why It Can Matter More Than IQ*. New York: Random House.

intelligence as being able to understand and interpret your motives and emotions and put yourself in another person's situation. If you learn to do that, you can be friends with people of almost all backgrounds, cultures, and trades.

Here's an example of what I mean. In 2016, I put myself in the position of a Trump voter during the US election, and I gained a lot of insights into Trump supporters' reasoning by engaging in many meaningful discussions. I agreed with many of their points and had respectful debates, but I also expressed my differing view that even if the establishment is a problem, Trump was not the solution. These debates deepened a few friendships and pushed me out of my social comfort zone. To develop emotional intelligence, engage with others different from yourself. It doesn't mean you have to change your opinion—I still think Trump was the wrong solution to the problem.

One of the most important benefits of my quest to achieve emotional intelligence has been my heartfelt and deeply personal discussions with people representing diverse political, sexual, and cultural backgrounds. Having a diverse set of friends is incredibly rewarding, and it certainly makes life a more colorful experience.

The biggest gain I received from studying and practicing emotional intelligence is the gift of being able to relate with people who disagree with me. When you stand in another person's shoes, you can see the world from their point of view. Your positions become more nuanced. You also learn not to envy others but to enjoy their success truly. You learn to empathize with their challenges. When you can relate, you will derive a lot more happiness and meaning from your encounters with friends, acquaintances, and colleagues.

Why I Wrote This Book

Over the years, I have spent a lot of time studying behavioral algorithms[5] and their impact on society and humanity. I've tested many algorithmic approaches to shaping behavior during that time with often mind-blowing results.

Maybe it's because of my knowledge and skills or my experiences, but I've grown increasingly downhearted about the current situation in social media. More often than not, we are shuttled from one echo chamber to the other without even realizing it. Our social media interactions are filtered into self-perpetuating bubbles that amplify our existing biases rather than allow us to understand other ideas. Where once the Internet was touted as breaking down walls and supporting open communication, too often, we are now fitted with blinders fashioned by behavioral algorithms.

The bubbles that social media constructs encourage tribal thinking–a natural, well-studied feature of human behavior that says when we join a group, we form ideas about and act in certain ways toward others in the group—the "in-group."

Conversely, we form attitudes toward and beliefs about people outside our group—the "out-group." It's us and them. It's us and "the others".[6]

Have you noticed that creating a healthy, constructive debate on almost any topic on social media has become next to impossible, as people from different sides mostly trade insults and jabs without trying to find any common ground? Almost anything you post results in some people canceling and blocking you. The real problem

---

[5] Algorithm is a process or set of rules to be followed in calculations or other problem-solving operations, especially by a computer.

[6] Tajfel, H. (1974). "Social identity and intergroup behavior". *Social Science Information*. 13 (2): 65–93.

with that isn't about your ego; it's that your social bubble becomes narrower every time someone with differing views cancels you.

These argumentative, divisive interactions are by design, not our own. Our worldview narrows every time we comment or react to a post, and algorithms reconfigure to feed us more of the same in a positive light (and consequently more of the opposite side in a negative light). We limit our learning potential by blocking people with different opinions. We lose our ability to negotiate and compromise and chances to learn emotional intelligence.

Some readers might argue that you can avoid the divisiveness designed into social networks by interacting with others in person. But that's not a panacea.

Decades-long social conditioning has also made it harder for us to debate in person. I find people jumping to conclusions on my positions based on their virtual reality filter bubble—whether or not we are talking face to face or through social networks.

What's worse, today's social media algorithms have turned a large portion of our youth into dopamine addicts with short attention spans, spending hours scrolling through a never-ending feed of bite-sized clips of entertainment. Most entertainers, or "influencers", do it for money and fame. Their occasional shares about good causes are overwhelmed with comments about unrealistic beauty standards, self-serving brags, and paid promotions that tap into and monetize our insecurities.

The culture we grow up in shapes us, and even if we walk away from our parents' belief systems, we still carry a unique set of views and values rooted in our youth. If we don't change the course, we risk ruining the lives of a whole generation. We need less mindless scrolling and more intellectual debate and healthy conversations.

Having deep conversations with others different from yourself can be hard, no matter where you have them. But I still love to debate with people from different backgrounds. I want to learn how they view the world and how their perspectives lead them to conclusions that differ from mine.

I have worked hard to build a network that spans filter bubbles and allows me to see different takes on the stories spreading through social media feeds. It has become increasingly challenging to build such a network. Algorithms don't have overt cultural origins. Their purpose is not to carry knowledge forward or to stay true to past experiences. Their purpose is to hook you on a content feed and maximize the social media platform's revenue by serving you many ads before you leave.

But we don't have to be passive and let ourselves be governed by algorithms. Like any tool, they can be studied and put to use for different purposes. Algorithms are tools that social networks use to drive engagement, a keyword for addiction. And if the way to keep you engaged is to stir up your emotions and put you into conflict with others, then that's what an algorithm will learn to do. But you can use that same design to turn an algorithm into a tool for influence and connection.

That's why I wrote this book—to show people that they can be in control of these algorithms and use the influence they build on social media for positive results. Those people, including you, can become Servant Influencers.

1

An Introduction

We Live in the Age of Artificial Intelligence

Google engineer Blake Lemoine stared at the screen before him. He had been having a conversation with LaMDA, Google's Language Model for Dialogue Applications, and it felt increasingly alive. As told by Nitasha Tiku in *The Washington Post*, he asked questions about religion, and the AI responded by talking about its rights and personhood. It appeared to fear death or being "turned off".[7]

Had the system become sentient? Had it developed consciousness? Did it have a sense of self? If the answers were "yes", then people needed to know. Lemoine thought LaMDA's AI might have reached a tipping point.

We live among technologies that can learn, make decisions, and maintain themselves. Relax–it's not a Skynet[8] that has become self-aware. We aren't rubbing shoulders with cyborgs. But shouldn't we

---

[7] Tajfel, H. (1974). "Social identity and intergroup behavior". *Social Science Information*. 13 (2): 65–93.*ost*, June 17, 2022.

[8] Skynet is a fictional artificial neural network-based conscious group mind and artificial general superintelligence system that serves as the antagonistic force of the Terminator movie franchise. It became self-aware in Terminator 2: Judgment Day.

be thinking about just how far along AI is in its development? Is it developing rational thought and emotional responses?

Lemoine took his concerns to Google's management. The ethics of AI are still being worked out. If the LaMDA AI had become sentient, Google would be opening Pandora's box comparable to cloning humans, genome editing, and a host of other issues that scientific advances have brought to light.

Google dismissed Lemoine's observations. The tech giant explained that an advanced chatbot is still just that—a chatbot. Data in, data out. But when does data exchange become indistinguishable from a human conversation? Lemoine worried that LaMDA's AI was getting uncomfortably close.

Google said there wasn't any evidence that the AI had achieved sentience. It was just very good at mimicking human interactions. Humans anthropomorphize all kinds of things. We talk to our pets; we name our cars. We talk back to the TV. It wasn't surprising to Google management or to Google research scientists that Lemoine had assigned the AI capacities it didn't possess.

Therefore, Lemoine went to the press, resulting in Google firing him for what it said violated its employment rules. Scores of ethicists in technology agree that LaMDA's AI and other iterations of artificial intelligence are nowhere close to consciousness. But I still feel sorry for Lemoine.

I have studied emotional intelligence as a hobby for a long time. Until recently, I believed emotional intelligence to remain one of the core advantages remaining to humans after artificial intelligence has taken over all tasks requiring memorization and logic. But AI languages like LaMDA and OpenAI's GPT are scarily advanced. And eventually, these AIs will start appearing emotionally intelligent. This can happen without them evolving any form of consciousness, as the technology is only mimicking human behavior and does not self-reflect in the same way we humans do. But if we respond as we would to another person, the consequences are the same.

I've studied and worked on emotionally intelligent algorithms for the past decade. For example, I worked with a world-class tech team to build a graph that mapped trust between people from online signals. We used machine learning to find the best person to introduce two people to add the maximum amount of trust to the introduction. The results we produced, coupled with results found in others' research, convinced me that people are no longer ahead of AI in applying emotional intelligence to build and improve human relationships.

Yuval Noah Harari writes in *Homo Deus* that humans are essentially a collection of biological algorithms shaped by millions of years of evolution[9]. He claims that there is no reason to think that non-organic algorithms couldn't replicate and surpass everything that organic algorithms can do.

Max Tegmark echoes the same in his book *Life 3.0: Being Human in the Age of Artificial Intelligence*[10]. He makes an interesting case that we can replicate practically all intelligence on other platforms outside the human brain. In that case, sensory information is not limited to human senses, and intelligence is not limited by the boundaries of the human brain.

Nothing is preventing an internet of connected computers from evolving a new artificial form of life that is superior to us.

Let that sink in for a moment. Our emotions and feelings are organic algorithms that respond to our environment. These

---

[9] Harari, Yuval Noah. 2017. *Homo Deus: A Brief History of Tomorrow*. Illustrated edition. New York, NY: Harper.
[10] Tegmark, Max. 2017. *Life 3.0: Being Human in the Age of Artificial Intelligence*. New York: Knopf.

algorithms are shaped by our cultural history, upbringing, and life experiences. And they can be reverse-engineered.

Harari, a professor at the Hebrew University of Jerusalem, and Tegmark, a professor at MIT in Boston, predict that computers will eventually become better at manipulating human emotions than humans themselves.

Generally speaking, people's emotional intelligence is often underdeveloped. Our biological systems produce default responses to many situations, freeing us to use our cognitive abilities elsewhere. In real-life situations, we often fail at using emotional intelligence. Overcoming our biological traits requires practice.

Most of us are ignorant about even the most basic emotional triggers we set off in others. We end up in pointless fights, dismiss good arguments because they go against our biases, and judge people based on stereotypes. For example, if we meet a person in religious clothing, we might assume their worldview to be our stereotypical view of that religion.

We don't understand the effects of cultural context, family upbringing, or the current personal life situation of the people we talk with. We rarely try to put ourselves in the other person's position. It's hard for us to understand their reasoning if it goes against our worldview. We don't want to challenge our biases or prejudices.

Online, the situation is much worse. We draw hasty and often mistaken conclusions from comments by people we don't know at all and lash out at them if their point goes against our biases.

Lastly, we often see life as the "survival of the fittest". This predisposes us toward taking advantage of others, boosting our egos, and putting ourselves on a pedestal.

Many successful people too often lie to gain an advantage, manipulate to get ahead and deceive to hide their wrongdoings. It's about winning at all costs, and it causes a lot of emotional damage along the way.

While we humans often struggle to understand each other, emotionally intelligent AI has advanced rapidly. Cameras in phones are ubiquitous and omnipresent, and face-tracking software is already advanced enough to analyze the smallest details of our facial expressions. The most advanced ones can even tell fake emotions from real ones. Generative[11] AIs can create believable texts and accurate "deepfake" images and videos of faces portraying any emotion.

Deepfakes are synthetic media in which a person in an existing image or video is replaced with someone else's likeness, such as digitally grafting someone's face on someone else's body. And they are uncannily accurate. The problem posed by deepfakes is obvious, as explained in a Brookings Institute report[12]: When we can't believe the images we see, we can no longer be spurred to action by emotionally connecting images like the one of the lone protester standing against the tanks in Tiananmen Square. Persuasion becomes more difficult because people reject what they see unless it comes from someone within their social media bubble.

In addition, voice recognition and natural language processing algorithms are getting better at figuring out our sentiment and

---

[11] Generative AI refers to unsupervised and semi-supervised machine learning algorithms that enable computers to use existing content like text, audio and video files, images, and even code to create new possible content. The main idea is to generate completely original artifacts that would look like the real deal.

[12] Galston, William A. 2020. "Is Seeing Still Believing? The Deepfake Challenge to Truth in Politics." Brookings (blog). January 8, 2020. https://www.brookings.edu/research/is-seeing-still-believing-the-deepfake-challenge-to-truth-in-politics/.

emotional state from both audio and text. These technologies that analyze emotional responses from faces and voices are already beyond the skills of an average person and often exceed the abilities of even the most skilled human beings. AI can look at our faces to recognize such private qualities as our sexual orientation, political leaning, or IQ.

Unlike people, AI can leverage your whole online history, which in most cases is more information than anybody can remember about any of their friends. Some of the most advanced machine learning algorithms developed at Meta and Google have already been applied to a treasure trove of data from billions of people.

The advances in this field are currently almost solely driven by commercial interests. Media and entertainment companies need our attention and engagement to make money. TikTok, Meta, and YouTube have large numbers of engineers working to create ever better ways to addict us to our content feeds.

These algorithms are designed to pull our emotional triggers to keep us entertained. And they have become very good at it. In a Guardian interview, Justin Rosenstein, a tech entrepreneur who led the Facebook team that created the Like button, said that he's worried about the power technology has on us and believes our minds can be hijacked. Rosenstein later starred in the documentary *The Social Dilemma* about the negative impacts of extended time spent on social networking platforms[13].

These algorithms know your desires, biases, and emotional triggers based on your communication, friends, and cultural context. In many areas, they understand you better than you know yourself.

The progress of algorithms has gone so far that Meta and Google have been accused of creating filter bubbles that affect public

---

[13] *The Social Dilemma - A Netflix Original Documentary.* n.d. The Social Dilemma. Accessed November 22, 2022. https://www.thesocialdilemma.com/.

opinion, rapidly changing political landscapes, and sway elections. Filter bubbles emerge when AI algorithms examine your reactions, posts, and other behavior to predict which content you will react to and like to feed you more of it. This strengthens your biases and lowers your ability to handle different points of view. These algorithms have grown so complex that they are becoming impossible to understand fully.

> ### The Future of Emotional Artificial Intelligence
>
> People have a lot of biases that cloud their judgment. We see the world as we wish it to be, not as it really is. Algorithms today, because they're designed by people, incorporate those same biases. If technology companies wanted to remove such biases from algorithms, it would be relatively easy to do. It hasn't happened yet because there isn't a business model that works with a healthier approach.

How Algorithms Use Us

In 2017, I predicted to my friends that we would see the first startup projects go from zero to unicorn (a billion-dollar valuation) in a week by the end of 2020. My friends laughed and said it would be impossible.

Yet it happened exactly as I predicted. Sushiswap is an automated cryptocurrency exchange running on the Ethereum blockchain. It launched on Aug 28th, 2020, and attracted $150 million during its first day. On Sept 1st, it was listed on Binance and FTX exchanges. By Sept 4th, it had attracted a total of $1.8 billion into its business.

At this point, some of my friends remembered my prediction. They asked me: "How on earth were you able to make such an accurate prediction?" It wasn't magic. For me, it was just simple math. I assumed that the size of the global cryptocurrency market would exceed one trillion dollars by the end of 2020. I also assumed that a top cryptocurrency project could attract 0.1% of the total market capitalization in one week.

While you can't define cryptocurrency projects as "unicorns" in the same way as startups with venture capital, the speed at which they can attract capital is impressive. How is it possible to attract so much money so fast?

The answer is *algorithmic incentives.* For example, smart contracts are software programs that run on top of blockchains to execute financial transactions between parties that don't know each other without the need for intermediaries. These programs often implement algorithmic financial incentives within cryptocurrency projects that automatically reward the earliest adopters the most for their participation. An interesting project can produce so much fear of missing out that the money floods like a tsunami. We could say that those algorithmic incentives "use us" to attract rapid funding for the project.

Incentives are not the only way that algorithms connect to us and use us to produce certain results. Targeting, search, feeds, and notifications also have roles.

How Algorithms Tap into Our Consciousness

API is a commonly used abbreviation for Application Programming Interface. In simple terms, APIs enable software applications to request information or perform tasks in other software applications.

The Internet is already full of APIs. They are used for everything imaginable: online shopping, payments, search, messaging, calls, advertising, and so on.

So far, APIs have been used to build connected services that help people use online services more effectively and transfer data between applications. APIs have been a way to unleash the power of data as a tool for us humans to be more productive. And now people have become APIs themselves–biology in service of technology.

How so? Let me explain. We are now at the point where algorithms drive the fastest growth and the largest profits for businesses. The use of algorithms allows companies to scale at a much, much faster rate than if relying solely on human labor.

As algorithms enable businesses to reach millions of people cost-effectively with individualized messages, business models have evolved from selling content into monetizing attention and engagement.

This evolution has given birth to a whole new class of developers whose job is to develop algorithms that grab your attention, keep you engaged, extract data about you, make you perform tasks, and convert you from being a free user to a paying customer. In short, these developers want to build an API to your mind.

And if you were a developer and wanted to influence people on a large scale via the human API, where would you start? There's only one right answer to this question. The ubiquitous, always-on, ever-present smartphone is such a powerful device for reaching people that you don't need anything else to grab their attention and influence their decisions.

In August 2022, according to Statista, there were over 6.5 billion smartphone users worldwide. That means well over 80% of the global population and almost everyone in the developed world has a smartphone. Over 60% of global web traffic is generated from smartphones[14].

The smartphone is currently the only always-on digital interface to your consciousness. Push notifications from smartphone applications tap into your senses of hearing, vision, and touch to grab your attention.

- **How Algorithms Gain Our Attention**

To start the process of turning humans into robots, you need their attention. And the best way to gain people's initial attention is to display a piece of content, either image, video, or text, on a social media feed or on a search results page.

A more aggressive way to grab their attention is to send them a cold message over chat or email. But this approach is risky and can backfire, causing anger and negative emotions among recipients. Both of the above strategies can be implemented with several currently available services, which are already connected to the APIs of major social networks, search engines, and message delivery services.

There still are numerous traditional strategies for gaining attention, such as TV, radio, newspapers, and outdoor ads, but they are not as scalable, measurable, and fast as online algorithmic models.

Importantly, the initial message must be tailored for the recipient, as different people have different interests. If you are looking for shortcuts, there are some time-tested strategies for general targeting.

---

[14] "Global Mobile Traffic 2022." n.d. Statista. Accessed November 7, 2022. https://www.statista.com/statistics/277125/share-of-website-traffic-coming-from-mobile-devices/.

For example, a picture of a beautiful woman in a bikini will generally attract the attention of the heterosexual adult male population. Videos of kittens and puppies will attract the attention of a large portion of both male and female populations.

However, while these shortcuts may get you the initial attention, they won't necessarily help you convert people for long-term engagement. If you desire the continuous attention of people, the initial message has to be related to the activity you wish to engage them in and to the results you wish to achieve with that engagement.

More importantly, your initial message has to motivate the targeted people to act in a desirable way—opt-in, purchase, join, download, donate, and so on.

Because the conversion rates from initial attention to these actions are low, this is a numbers game. Your algorithms have to continuously send different messages, testing various content and channel strategies to maximize the conversion rates for each target demography.

In the age of instant gratification, we have become restless and impatient. Social media apps do their best to gain users at least a few likes and comments from their friends as quickly as possible. Those engagements are sent to you over notifications to pull you back to the conversation.

Those notification bubbles on top of the app icons, aren't they enticing? It's hard not to become addicted to checking out what has happened in your circles while you were out. The genius of the notification bubbles is their ability to lure you in, even if you don't have push notifications turned on for those apps.

Today's smartphone notifications use three of the human senses. They beep, they vibrate, and they show the notification on the phone screen. Developers leverage smartphone notifications to lure you back over and over again.

But this result is increasingly hard to achieve. People are quick to reject notification access and slow to allow it. If your algorithm sends notifications that people don't like, they will not only block the notifications but also likely delete your app altogether.

There are two effective strategies that can be deployed in algorithms to gain notification access. The first is to use an existing messaging app for which people have already enabled notifications. This is the best way forward if the goal is to get users to follow you, join a community chat, or add a service bot[15] to an existing messaging or social media app.

The second strategy is to get the person to install an app that independently initiates notifications. Algorithms can increase their chances of getting app notifications enabled if they are related to messaging. The desire to receive messages from other people, for example, will motivate your app users to enable notifications.

Once allowed, notifications can be extremely effective in grabbing the user's full attention and hanging on to it. Now the company designing the algorithm stands to benefit from this gained attention.

There are currently three main methods to monetize engagement. You can extract behavioral data from users, make users work for you, or make users pay you. The following sections describe each of these methods.

---

[15] Chatbot: a computer program designed to simulate conversation with human users, especially over the internet.

- **How Algorithms Extract Behavioral Data**

Behavioral data, like the online interactions of your prospective and current customers, is valuable. It can be sold to advertisers and businesses who can offer services based on that data. To successfully capture personal data, it's important to understand that incentives are a key enabler. People can be incentivized with money, fame, and social approval. Offering real-world money, fame, or social approval is challenging, but there's a trick: the incentives don't have to be real, they can be virtual.

Game developers figured this out a long time ago, and they make billions with algorithms that reward people with virtual money, virtual fame, and virtual social approval.

Virtual rewards work amazingly well for soliciting user-generated content. For example, Facebook algorithms make sure that each wall post gets a few likes almost instantly to provide people with virtual social approval. That keeps people hooked and makes it hard to build less addicting alternatives.

The virtual fame reward is perfected in Quora, which offers "Top Writer in #insert-your-topic" badges to people who contribute popular answers to a specific topic. For the folks who contribute the most, they even send a branded jacket.

You can extract almost any information from people if your algorithms provide them with proper virtual rewards. For example, if you want to extract the health data of users, the best strategy is to capture the information passively via wearable sensors that they wear–think FitBit, Apple Watch, and others. You can only keep gathering data from wearables over longer periods of time if you offer proper virtual rewards like achievements, streaks, and useful statistics.

Not all rewards associated with algorithms have to be virtual. You can also provide real rewards. Using cryptocurrencies can provide real monetary rewards algorithmically to people for their data. The value of these rewards depends on the market value of the cryptocurrency being used.

- **How Algorithms Put Us to Work**

Some businesses monetize their users by making them work. This requires real monetary rewards, as people need to pay for their food, clothes, and shelter. But the required rewards are typically low and can usually be monetized at a higher rate for profit.

Uber is a great example of a successful implementation of the concept. Uber's algorithms send a notification to nearby drivers when a ride becomes available and provides drivers with the optimal route for picking up and dropping off their riders. You could think of this arrangement as managing a human robot to move the car to the desired location.

Another successfully implemented algorithmic task delivery system is Amazon Mechanical Turk. You can use that platform to send almost any task to hundreds of thousands of people all over the world. Because many people compete for the task, you usually get the job done quickly for pennies. Online shipment and food delivery platforms also leverage this method.

- **How Algorithms Trigger People to Pay**

Kensgold, a 19-year-old Reddit user, was not a typical gambler. But he still managed to lose $13,500 in a myriad of microtransactions over several online games.[16] Any individual transaction is so small it hardly draws attention. But the game's

---

[16] "Meet The 19-Year-Old Who Spent Over $10,000 On Microtransactions." n.d. Accessed January 6, 2023. https://kotaku.com/meet-the-19-year-old-who-spent-over-10-000-on-microtra-1820854953.

design, supported by well-honed algorithms, smoothed over any natural hesitation to spend. Game developers have long used behavioral designs that leverage timely psychological triggers to push users to make these small purchases. Players are programmed to keep playing and spending–beat the next boss, reach the next level, heal faster, find a better weapon.

Kensgold's open letter to game developers–some of the biggest names in the business–identified his enemy. He had a full-blown gambling addiction—lured into spending small amounts of money to keep playing, progressing, and rising higher on the leaderboards. From the moment he was 13, the game algorithms gradually turned him into an addict. Kensgold was what the gaming industry calls a "whale"—one of those players whose microtransactions make up the lion's share of the industry's revenue.

Kensgold did find the help he needed to break the habit he'd built over years of game-playing. With a therapist's help, he learned to keep the purchase triggers in games at a distance. He still makes microtransactions, but when he does, he's mindful of the dangers. He knows how to identify how games encourage virtual spending, and he avoids those games now–even if his friends don't. He hopes his experience will help other players avoid the fate he created for himself.

It's not only the games industry that has perfected monetization through behavioral algorithms. Many successful companies have automated their monetization. When algorithms capture data from a social media platform, that data can be automatically monetized by selling it to the highest bidding advertisers. This strategy generates billions of dollars in profits for companies like Meta, YouTube, LinkedIn, Twitter, and many others.

When algorithms are monetized through crowdsourced work, that labor is usually pre-sold to others at a premium. This strategy is used by companies like Amazon, Uber, Delivery Hero, Takeaway, DoorDash, and many others.

Subscription services such as Spotify and Netflix extract behavioral data to learn as much as possible about their users and then deliver suggestions of content they might like to ensure people continue paying for a premium subscription.

Now you understand how businesses leverage algorithms to generate billions in profits without the need for human labor beyond engineering resources. This is the future of business and leaves us with this troubling question:

How many companies we just talked about have already hooked us?

How Algorithms Shape Our Societies

Throughout human history, cultures have evolved and spread through memes[17], which are cultural analogs to genes. Memes shape our cultural evolution. Some memes are broadcast faster and wider than others, creating unique narratives for different cultures, societies, and faiths.

This process is much like the biological evolution and the survival of the fittest concept that has shaped our species and evolved people in different areas of the world to have different characteristics.

The survival of the fittest memes is why we still have rich narratives about the big battles and other major historical events recorded in books, but not so many details about ordinary events of those times.

---

[17] Meme is an idea, behavior, or style that spreads from person to person within a culture—often with the aim of conveying a particular phenomenon, theme, or meaning.

- **The Impact of Broadcast Media**

The rise of broadcast media from the early 1900s enabled us to participate collectively in important historical moments. Profound radio or TV speeches by leaders like Winston Churchill, John F. Kennedy, or Ronald Reagan unified or rallied whole nations.

Broadcast media also made it possible to capture the public imagination and shape national culture. Hollywood movies and popular TV shows have had a lasting impact not only on American culture but on other cultures across the world.

In its early days, the curation of content by major broadcast corporations and governments amounted to massive, collective brainwashing. Communist and capitalist countries captured their people's imaginations with prime-time TV. The content of communist regimes was created and selected to shape public opinion. On the other hand, the content in capitalist countries was broadcasted based on its potential to make money.

Depending on the era and the political system, this top-down curation either enforced the dominant culture or pushed new memes and values to the mainstream. The American TV of the 1950s popularized domestic comedy series, which promoted an ideal of a suburban white nuclear family with kids and a housewife.

In the 1960s, increased violence and global threats discussed in the news were countered with TV series focused on fantasy escapism. In the 1970s, traditional family values were replaced with racial and cultural diversity. The 1980s brought a major growth of violence in TV, movies, and popular video games, resulting in an average American kid seeing 16,000 murders and 200,000 acts of violence by the time they turn 18[18].

---

[18] Muscari M. 2002. "Media Violence: Advice for Parents." *Pediatr Nurs.* 28(6):585-91. PMID: 12593343.

Between 1950 and 1990, American culture evolved from an idealized "nuclear suburban white family life" to include and accommodate diversity. At the same time, the tolerance for violence increased significantly, with most children exposed to insane amounts of violent content during their childhoods.

- **The Internet Years**

From the 1990s onward, the Internet entered and grew in popular culture, and TV gained a formidable competitor for people's time and attention. TV channels started specializing and catering to a myriad of narrow niches.

The shows' TV hosts and main characters started including people from niche cultures, including the rise of Ellen DeGeneres as the first openly gay TV show host in the late 1990s. The show initially drew much controversy and was canceled, but it returned to TV later as a highly successful long-term show.

Since the late 1990s, we've seen a massive rise in reality TV, where normal people were encouraged to compete in various settings. Over time, this led to people doing more and more controversial things for the viewers' entertainment. Every time there was a new controversy, viewer ratings tended to spike. As the ratings directly affected the advertising revenue, reality TV became a race to the bottom.

- **Social Media Changed Everything**

During the 2000s, social media entered the mainstream. It changed the way we received and consumed our information. Instead of the daily serving of mainstream broadcasts, we started seeing content curated and personalized to us using algorithms.

This might sound good, but we must understand how the algorithm works before making judgments. All mainstream social media companies are in business to generate a return for their investors, and the money comes almost solely from their advertisers.

Former Facebook executive Eugene Wei blogged once that people are status-seeking monkeys. He identifies utility, entertainment, and social capital as the main contributors to the success of a social network[19].

The business of social networks is to convert this social capital and utility into a financial return. The goal of social feed algorithms is to maximize advertising revenue. To achieve this goal, social media platforms need to maximize their membership's engagement, or rather, addiction, to their algorithmic feeds.

So how do you hook people into spending time on your page or app? Addiction algorithms are already so well understood and implemented by the games industry that by 2018, all of the top-grossing games on the Google Play store had "addictive" listed as the most used word in their ratings.

AI makes it possible to mass customize the addiction models to each individual. Once you have learned the types of content the person likes, you serve them a constant stream of dopamine hits with instant gratifications within their interests.

Another powerful way to keep people hooked is to appeal to their vices. If you think about it, at least one social media platform already catered to all of our vices.

So how do the addiction-oriented algorithms of the major social media platforms affect our cultural evolution? Let me explain.

---

[19] "Status as a Service (StaaS)." n.d. Remains of the Day. Accessed January 4, 2023. https://www.eugenewei.com/blog/2019/2/19/status-as-a-service.

- **The Spread of Social Media Memes**

To maximize views of advertisements, the social network has to attract enough user-generated content that the members stay hooked. This is where the algorithms turn evil.

The centrally curated memes we received earlier from broadcast media have been replaced with a cacophony of social media memes curated by everyone. A massive low-quality information overload is being filtered by algorithms that optimize for the total viewing time, not for the truth value of the content.

Under this constant and heavy bombardment of distractions, our attention spans have shrunk to a few seconds. A video view is counted at 3 seconds, and they auto-play when you pass them in the feed. Why? Because most people drop out early, and the networks need big numbers to attract advertisers.

Instead of providing context and helping us navigate important issues, profit-optimizing algorithms direct our attention to pointless dopamine loops that last a few seconds each. The hope is that we engage enough to drop the like before we scroll further.

Instagram has optimized this loop to perfection. Scroll, double-tap, scroll, double-tap, repeat. You know the drill.

What Went Wrong?

Dopamine-driven content consumption has changed the way people grow their influence. You don't succeed on social media by offering substance, writing quality posts, or speaking the truth. You succeed by sharing bold, crazy, but most of all, meme-worthy content. Truth be damned. Donald Trump won the US presidency partly because his tweets were the most meme-worthy ones that consistently went viral, keeping him in the spotlight at all times.

This is why misinformation and disinformation spread so fast. It doesn't matter whether the story is true; the criteria for its spread is its meme-worthiness, not its content.

I have studied and written about emotionally intelligent algorithms for a number of years now. Once I figured out how they worked, I tested my assumptions many times by posting content that I thought could go viral and optimizing everything for the algorithm. It wasn't long before I had over a million monthly viewers for my posts. People on top of their game on social networks respect the algorithm, meaning they don't try to go against it. They serve content that the algorithms prefer. Unfortunately, sharing high-quality opinions gains you less visibility than timely memes.

If they want, social media companies can manipulate our worldviews through their algorithms. These algorithms can sway elections. They can divide nations. They can pick the winners and losers on the altar of public opinion. But it's important to understand that most manipulation happens as an unintended consequence of the social feed algorithms trying to maximize the addiction and the profits.

As natural-language AIs approach human skill levels, our ability to distinguish the objective truth from a sea of manipulation, disinformation, and misinformation is diminished. We have entered an era in which AI can affect the common narratives of our cultural evolution by making generating personalized messages extremely scalable.

Even so, nobody would submit an AI-composed academic article to a peer-reviewed journal, right? Publishing in academic journals is notoriously difficult and laborious, even for the most earnest scholar.

But Almira Osmanovic Thunström wondered. So she asked GPT-3 (an advanced AI language model capable of producing text that reads as if written by humans) to write 500 words about itself, including citations and references. Astounded at the results, Thunström expanded her experiment, directing GPT-3 to write a full article to answer the question: Can someone publish a paper from a nonhuman source[20]?

As Hannah Getahun of *The Washington Post* tells it, GPT-3 wrote its article in less than two hours, and Thunström began the submission process. She asked for and received GPT-3's permission to publish, and the AI testified it had no conflicts of interest that precluded publication–standard submission practices at peer-reviewed journals. Thunström completed the submission process and now had a near-complete answer to her question[21].

Apparently, GPT-3's paper could be submitted, but a human intervention was needed for management chores such as submitting an author name, identifying whom to contact for revisions, and so on. Nevertheless, scores of ethical and scientific, and editorial questions are raised by her experiment.

If an AI-generated academic research article is accepted by a peer-reviewed journal, how can everyday media consumers identify whether the stories they read are the result of human observation or are written by an AI? Just imagine all the possible ways artificial intelligence can manipulate us by mimicking human behavior. You can already use it to respond to, amplify, debate, and react to human communication on social media at a massive scale.

Can anything be done to change the course of social media?

---

[20] Thunström, Almira Osmanovic. n.d. "We Asked GPT-3 to Write an Academic Paper about Itself;Then We Tried to Get It Published." *Scientific American.* Accessed October 14, 2022.

[21] Getahun, Hannah. n.d. "After an AI Bot Wrote a Scientific Paper on Itself, the Researcher behind the Experiment Says She Hopes She Didn't Open a 'Pandora's Box.'" *Insider.* Accessed October 14, 2022. https://www.insider.com/artificial-intelligence-bot-wrote-scientific-paper-on-itself-2-hours-2022-7.

Yes, at least temporarily. First, we can find alternative ways to finance social media platforms so that they do not need to addict us and then manipulate us to make money. That's a tall order, but the decentralized models that Telegram tried to implement and Mastodon is currently implementing could help us get there.

Second, we will need to verify social media accounts to improve the quality of the conversation and increase trust between the participants. Elon Musk, for one, understands this. After he acquired Twitter in the fall of 2022, he initiated a project to verify a larger portion of Twitter users in exchange for a fee, aiming to increase Twitter's revenue outside advertising.

Unfortunately, being able to pay to verify one's identity led to widespread impersonation and general chaos. Therefore, Elon quickly paused the service to improve the identity verification processes.

Now that you have a basic understanding of social media algorithms, it is time to start the journey toward becoming a servant influencer. In the next chapter, I will discuss how to choose the right platform and build the right kind of network.

2

How to Make Friends and Gain Followers

As a young entrepreneur from a small country, Finland, I dreamed of living in Silicon Valley and building startups there. In 2007, after we had sold our Berlin-based mobile games startup, I realized this dream and moved my family of five to Foster City, California. It is a town by the water, conveniently located between Palo Alto and San Francisco.

It didn't take me long to realize why the San Francisco Bay Area had become the center of gravity in the startup world. Successful entrepreneurs from all over the world had moved there and were networking, sharing ideas, and testing each other's early products. At networking events, people were accessible and helpful.

Before I moved in, I had already spent a lot of time in Silicon Valley. I remember playing arcade games in a Palo Alto cafe with Michael Arrington, the founder of "TechCrunch", with me being one of the earliest readers. I had dinner with Drew Houston, the founder of Dropbox, gave feedback to Mark Zuckerberg on his new product concept, and petted the dog of the late Ted Rheingold, the founder of Dogster while talking with him and Mark Pincus, the founder of Zynga. Of course, this all happened before these famous entrepreneurs reached the pinnacle of their success, and we were all working on building something that we found meaningful.

The Silicon Valley network effect worked so that new product releases were first distributed among fellow local entrepreneurs, mostly immigrants with large followings in their home countries. When they shared about those cool new products on their social media walls, they created early traction for their friends' startups by reaching large audiences in their home countries.

The global Covid-19 pandemic changed this dynamic. Living in Silicon Valley is no longer necessary to build a strong network. You can build that directly on social media. You just have to find the right communities and build affinity with their members. But how do you find the right circles where future star entrepreneurs and thought leaders hang? And how do you get accepted into such communities? By being friends with their friends. In this chapter, I will discuss how you can build the right network for your goals.

Choose a Platform Based on Your Goals

You can't effectively build influence in all of the social networks at the same time. Not if you want to be good at it. You have to choose the platform based on your goals, and there are many important criteria to account for. If you were to develop a strategy for that purpose, you'd ask yourself the following questions:

- Are you planning to build an audience or a community?
- Which networking model matches your purpose?
- Which platforms are popular among your target demographic?
- What kind of identity should you adopt?

I will help you answer these questions in the following chapters.

Are You Building an Audience or a Community?

Many people confuse the terms audience and community. Companies might hire community managers to help message their audience, and influencers may call their audience a "community".

When you or your company shares something, and others react to it, we are talking about an audience. Instagram account is an audience. Facebook page is an audience. TikTok or YouTube channel is an audience. Each share is a one-to-many broadcast with the influencer at the center of attention.

When a group of people comes together to jointly further a shared interest, you have a community. In a community, many people share, and members help each other to succeed. A Facebook group could be a community. Discord is a community platform. WhatsApp is a community platform.

In other words, some social platforms are great for audience building, while others focus on community building. First, you have to decide what you want to build—thought leadership for yourself or a community around your business or cause. It's exceedingly hard to build thought leadership for a company account, so I don't recommend trying to do that.

Which Networking Model Matches Your Purpose?

Each type of social network has a different model of operation, which affects how you can build your influence there. Take time to examine social networks in terms of how their models fit your goals and purpose. Five main networking models have developed throughout social network evolution: the friend model, the follower model, the interest-based model, the group model, and, most recently, the algorithmic model.

TYPES OF SOCIAL MEDIA PLATFORMS

	in	f	🐦	🐘	💬	#	🔴	▶	📷	👻	Q
REAL IDENTITY	X	X	X	X	X	X		X	X	X	X
PSEUDONYMOUS			X	X	X	X	X	X	X	X	
FRIEND MODEL	X	X			X	X				X	
FOLLOWER MODEL	X	X	X	X			X		X	X	X
GROUP MODEL	X	X			X	X	X			X	X
INTEREST-BASED MODEL							X				X
ALGORITHMIC MODEL								X	X		

- LinkedIn
- Slack
- Facebook
- Reddit
- Twitter
- YouTube
- Mastodon
- Instagram
- WhatsApp
- TikTok
- Telegram
- Snapchat
- Discord
- Quora

Friend Model

The Friend model is probably the model you're most familiar with, used in the early days of Facebook, LinkedIn, and others–what you might call the "first wave" of social network evolution. They're excellent platforms for building personal relationships and enhancing your reputation. On Facebook, for example, you can have public conversations with your friends on your wall and engage in private conversations through messaging. The benefit of the Friend model is that it offers direct messaging access to people who choose to accept your connection. LinkedIn functions in a similar way. The connections are valuable because they open direct communication channels with other users, enabling you to build more personal relationships.

Follower Model

The second wave of social networking arrived with Twitter and Instagram and brought with it the Follower model. This model concentrates influence in the hands of a relatively small number of people and leaves the rest of the users in the role of content consumers. As a consumer in this scenario, you follow someone, but they rarely follow you in return. It's hard to build a network because a mutual connection isn't required, and the personal relationship between the followers and the influencers is shallow or non-existent. However, if you are able to become an influencer on these platforms, or if you are a celebrity bringing your followers on these platforms, you can shape opinions and behavior on a large scale.

Interest-Based Model

Reddit and Quora are examples of the rise of interest-based networking, where following and friending have become secondary to the discussion topics. On platforms deploying the Interest model, you discover and follow the content you're interested in. Creating an interesting feed for yourself is easy because all you need to do is click and follow topics. Unlike the Friend model, you don't have to wait for someone to accept your invitation to connect. However, the driving force is the topic around which discussion forms. Importantly to the servant influencer: even if you can dominate a topic, you won't have direct access to the topic's following. The emphasis remains on the topic, not the people who joined the conversation. And that emphasis makes it hard to build relationships.

Group Model

Group networking became an integral part of social networking with the rise of Facebook Groups, Telegram, Discord, and Slack. The group model brings people with a common interest into a synchronous real-time conversation. That boosts building real-world relationships, and if you use your real identity, you can also build a professional reputation on these platforms.

The Group model differs from the Interest model in that you look for communities of interest rather than topics of interest and then request to join those communities. Depending on your level of participation and the value other community members place on your contributions, you can gain respect inside the communities you join. Usually, you can access community members via direct messaging. That gives you intimacy and the ability to build influence among a small group of people.

However, the model has drawbacks when it comes to building influence, depending on how the platform implements the model.

For example, topics on Slack and Discord can often be ephemeral. It's very hard to build any kind of meaningful content trail that can be traced back to you as a person. Building longer-term thought leadership remains difficult without direct recognition of the members due to anonymity or the absence of a content trail due to the ephemeral nature of those channels.

An important promise of the Group model is that real-time communication enables you to build trust with other members. However, trust is inversely correlated with the size of the community. The smaller the group, the more intimacy and trust there is.

> ## Why Facebook Business Groups Beat Out LinkedIn Business Groups
>
> Facebook groups used to be the best way to build business-related communities. For example, Tesla successfully based their marketing strategy on activating customers to share on social media through Tesla clubs on Facebook instead of spending on paid advertising.
>
> Did you ever wonder why Facebook groups were so popular among business people while LinkedIn groups had significantly lower engagement? It's because LinkedIn hasn't mastered the notification game for their groups.
>
> Since its launch in 2010, Facebook Groups implemented notifications so well that it was easily the best place to build any business-related community during the decade that followed. You could get multiple times more engagement in a Facebook group than in any competing alternative.
>
> In the early 2020s, Facebook's popularity waned, which prompted Meta to invest in WhatsApp's group functionality to avoid losing community builders to other platforms.

Algorithmic Model

We're now well into the algorithmic model of social networking, the most recent step in social media evolution. YouTube was the first mostly algorithmic social media platform, but TikTok is the poster child for this model. In this model, you consume content, and the next piece of content automatically displays to you based on your current and historical reactions to the already displayed content.

Both TikTok and YouTube allow you to subscribe to your favorite creators. But the auto-play (YouTube) and for-you-page (TikTok) algorithms give a real viral lift to the content that attracts reactions. So, the success of your posts depends on how well you can tap into the viral undercurrents inside the algorithms.

The viral aspect of the algorithm can't be overstated in terms of building an audience. You can create content that travels extremely far and wide based on initial reactions and interactions. Compare that to the friend model: initially, your friends react, which makes the content visible to the friends of friends. To make content viral, it has to be public. The follower model works the same way. With an algorithmic model, the audience can expand explosively without going through a jungle of connections.

Whatever platform you choose, remember who your closest professional friends and allies are. Even if you work on other models than group networking, try to establish a safe space online for sharing and conversations with them. That is the surest road to building trust and relationships. We'll return to this idea in later chapters when you begin to use influence to create opportunities and communities.

Where Is Your Target Audience?

Each social media has its own user demographic. LinkedIn is popular among professionals. Snapchat, Instagram, and TikTok appeal to younger generations, while Facebook appeals to older generations. Discord is popular among gamers and crypto/NFT enthusiasts. In contrast, Twitter is where people get news, and Mastodon has early appeal to those who think social media should not be owned by any centralized entity. When you are choosing your platform, look at the popularity of each platform among your target audience. The platform popularity sets the upper limit of your network size.

But you can't make this decision in isolation. Your goals also require a decision on the networking model andbetween building an audience or a community.

Should I Reveal My Identity?

Maybe you haven't thought about whether to use a pseudonymous identity or your real-world identity while building your online influence. But you should. On the one hand, how can you influence others when they don't know who you are? But, on the other hand, what risks do you take in using your real identity? The answers often connect to the goal you set and the platform you chose.

Facebook and LinkedIn, for example, have a real-name policy to ensure authenticity on their platforms. But disclosing your real identity can lead to harassment, cancel mobs, political oppression, and pose a real risk to your life and well-being.

According to studies, pseudonymity can lead to less aggressive stances, higher engagement, and higher-quality conversations. But at the same time, the reports indicated that pseudonymity could erode the community spirit when some users are aggressive toward others because aggressors aren't easily identified. In addition, Bots, trolls, and other disinformation spreaders flourish when platforms allow pseudonymity.

If you want to build influence that leads to life-changing opportunities, you must do it with your real identity. Even if you have a "stage name," connect it openly to a real identity. However, if you want to rally people to a cause, be mindful of your safety and potential consequences. You can make yourself a target by using a real identity. If you're part of a minority group under oppression from a hostile home government, you don't want to make it easy for the government to target you. If you live in an unsafe society, you don't want mobs or factions to target you, either.

Use Goals as Guides

Four goals fall under my definition of a servant influencer. Plenty of other goals fall outside the servant influencer, including one very common: You want to become famous. If you want to become famous for the sake of being famous, you can do that. But this book is not targeted at you. Instead, this book focuses on helping you help others. That's the path toward making a bigger impact in your life—by helping others make an impact in theirs. It's a road that runs through authenticity, influence, and community. When those three elements combine, positive change becomes possible.

For each of the goal categories below, you can achieve results using this book's ideas, guidance, and vision:

1. You are an entrepreneur on a mission.

2. You are a creator and want to make a difference.

3. You want to advocate a cause that you deeply care about.

4. You want to learn and educate people.

Reaching your goal is a process, not a switch. This book gives you access to that process.

You can use these four goal categories to learn about the choices you might make to select the most suitable social network for your efforts. Your selection within these categories will reflect which social media model serves your goal best, who are the people who can help you achieve your goal, and where you can find those people.

The Entrepreneur

	in	f	y	@	©	✈	💬	👍	▶	⊙	👻	Q
B2B SALES-LED GROWTH	X											
B2B PRODUCT-LED GROWTH	X	X	X	X	X	X		X				X
B2C SALES-LED GROWTH	X	X								X		
B2C PRODUCT-LED GROWTH	X	X	X	X					X	X	X	
MARKETPLACE	X	X	X	X	X	X	X	X	X	X	X	X
WEB3 / NFT / CRYPTO			X	X	X	X	X	X				
BUILD A COMMUNITY		X				X	X					

Mastodon profile is based on current trends.

Most entrepreneurs are known for being creative and innovative. They are willing to take risks and aren't discouraged by failures. Instead, they see failures as opportunities to learn and grow. This ability to quickly adapt and learn from mistakes is an important trait for entrepreneurs. Therefore, when choosing a social network platform for their business, entrepreneurs need to carefully consider which platform will give them the best return on their efforts. This will involve researching the different options and analyzing the potential benefits and drawbacks.

Let's say you're the founder of a B2B startup with a sales-led growth model, meaning that you're mostly targeting corporate accounts with big deals. When you look at the social media platform landscape, there's really no alternative to choosing LinkedIn based on your goal.

What if you're trying to grow a self-service product business and want to build brand awareness for your products and services? In this case, your personal relationships do not scale anymore. Instead, you want people to be interested in what you have to offer so that you can convert that interest into sales. For this news, you can use a wider range of social media platforms to promote your brand and reach more potential customers.

Depending on your product category, you could use Twitter, Facebook, or YouTube to build an audience for your product. Why these? Because for self-service B2B products, your audience is likely still professionals, but you don't need to build personal connections with every customer.

The demographics of social network platforms other than these three are not as good a match for what you need. Now, you could build a community around your products and services on Slack. The problem is that it is very hard to build an active community on Slack because people use it mostly as a company's internal communication platform. Discord is better for community building, but for B2B products, the fit is not great because Discord's main user base is gamers, developers, and crypto/NFT enthusiasts.

But what if you offer B2C products or services? The best platform for you depends on the type of your product or service. For example, LinkedIn might still be a good network for you if you focus on selling large-ticket consumer products like houses or cars. But you might be better served using Instagram or Facebook to reach a broad audience and more abundant opportunities. Users on those two platforms represent a wide demographic and are available to you to shape your most meaningful networks.

It's a different story if you're offering low-ticket consumer goods. In that case, you'll want to use such tactics as influencer marketing on TikTok, YouTube, Snapchat, or Instagram. In this case, you can also take other approaches, including paid advertising on most major networks. For example, Reddit would be an excellent place to promote Robinhood, a stock-trading app for young traders. On Reddit, there's a massive trader group called r/wallstreetbets, which has over 13 million members and emerged as a lucrative source of growth for Robinhood. Reddit users' anonymity is not a big deal here because stock traders usually prefer to remain anonymous towards their counterparties.

If you are a web3 entrepreneur working on a cryptocurrency or NFT project, your choices are more limited. Most social networks don't accept crypto ads, so your best bet is to build an active community on Reddit, Telegram, or Discord and incentivize the community members to promote your cause. You might now wonder why I mention cryptocurrency projects, often seen as scams or pyramid schemes, in a book about being a servant influencer!

The truth is many good impact projects are being built as web3 projects. I have personally helped multiple such impact projects focusing on solving one or several of the United Nations sustainable development goals (SDGs).

The Creator

	in	f	y	@	◎	✈	💬	👽	▶	📷	🔔	Q
TEXT-CENTRIC	X	X	X	X								X
STILL IMAGES-CENTRIC		X								X		
VIDEO-CENTRIC		X							X	X	X	
AUDIO-CENTRIC									X			
BUILD A COMMUNITY		X				X	X	X				

In November 2021, Illia Ponomarenko, a Ukrainian journalist, found himself unemployed. He was fired, together with his colleagues, from his job at the Kyiv Post, the largest English-language newspaper in Ukraine. That was the start of the Kyiv Independent[22].

The reporters had no funding or resources, but people loved them so much that they got their first office space, legal services, and hosting for free. A couple of months later, Russia invaded Ukraine. Illia, who calls himself "a village guy from Donbas", started sharing relatable and often emotional stories of the war on Twitter.

He quickly became the person to follow for English-language commentary on the war in Ukraine. He went from ten thousand

---

[22] D'Agostino, Susan. 2022. "Illia Ponomarenko: Ukraine's Most-Followed War Journalist Is a 'Dude' from Donbas." Bulletin of the Atomic Scientists (blog). April 28, 2022. https://thebulletin.org/2022/04/illia-ponomarenko-ukraines-most-followed-war-journalist-is-a-dude-from-donbas/.

followers to a million followers rapidly. As a defense reporter, he became bigger than most newspapers.

Illia hasn't wasted his newfound popularity. He has tirelessly promoted charities and organized fundraisers for various humanitarian causes.

A writer, videographer, musician, photographer, engineer, or any other kind of creative professional you want to name has different measures of success than an entrepreneur, even though creators share plenty of traits with entrepreneurs (creativity being one of them). In this particular instance, the focus is on a creator who wants to share their passion with the world. They hope to attract people who will look to them for ideas and inspiration—even participation. Often, a creator will look at social networks from a perspective linked to the content form in which they work.

For example, suppose your creative work is best presented with audio, video, or images. In that case, you can build a presence on networks like Instagram, Snapchat, TikTok, YouTube, and even, to some extent, on LinkedIn, Facebook, or Twitter. If you're a writer and your content is mostly text, your options are more limited. The top three social media platforms for attracting an audience would be Facebook, Twitter, and LinkedIn. You could also try to build a blog or a newsletter.

The Advocate

	in	f	🐦	@	🟢	✈	💬	🔴	▶	🎵	📷	👻	Q
SOCIAL JUSTICE	X	X	X	X	X	X		X	X	X			
CLIMATE / ENVIRONMENT	X	X	X	X	X	X		X	X	X			
HOBBIES		X		X	X	X	X	X	X	X	X		X
CRYPTO / NFT			X		X	X	X	X					
BUILD A COMMUNITY		X		X	X	X							

Sitting alone outside a government building on Fridays with a protest sign might not sound like a powerful way to gain visibility. But that doesn't mean it can't be effective. And you have to start somewhere.

In 2018 at age 15, Greta Thunberg sat outside the Swedish parliament building and wielded a single placard: School Strike for Climate. Her – or her social media team's – incredible meme powers on social networks combined with mainstream media coverage launched her climate change protest worldwide. Now a renowned Swedish climate advocate, she speaks at international conferences and has famously dressed down the government and corporate leaders for their lack of climate-crisis action.

The world has no shortage of just causes that need support. From climate change to political repression to justice and equality, every cause brings its champions. If you're one of them, then the strategies and information in this book may be especially meaningful.

Advocating for a cause is a special case in which you must pay attention to the matter of pseudonyms or real identity. Some advocacy work, such as Greta Thunberg's work on climate change, benefits from her identifying herself on social media. It adds credibility to her cause, gives her audience a human connection they can support, and makes it easier to expand her reach beyond social network platforms to legacy media such as television and print. But there is other advocacy work in which sharing your real identity could put you in danger or have other negative repercussions, as I mentioned earlier. We live in an AI-powered surveillance society, and it's hard enough to guard your privacy when you're online (relative to where you live and whether your government respects your privacy rights). Either way, you don't want to make it easy for your enemies to harass you or worse.

The Educator

	LinkedIn	Facebook	Twitter	Mastodon	WhatsApp	Telegram	Discord	Slack	YouTube	Instagram	TikTok	Snapchat	Quora
TECHNICAL TOPICS	X		X	X	X	X	X	X					X
BUSINESS TOPICS	X	X	X			X	X		X				X
FINANCIAL TOPICS	X	X	X			X	X	X	X				X
LEADERSHIP TOPICS	X	X	X			X	X		X				X
ARTS, DESIGN & CRAFTS		X			X	X	X			X	X	X	X
BUILD A COMMUNITY		X				X	X						

Tim Ferriss, a world-famous author and podcaster made his breakthrough with his bestseller book, *The 4-Hour Workweek*[23]. But

---

[23] Ferriss, Timothy. 2009. *The 4-Hour Workweek: Escape 9-5, Live Anywhere, and Join the New Rich*. Expanded and Updated ed., 1st revised ed. New York: Crown Publishers.

it wasn't an accidental win. Tim started blogging in 2006 and actively built his social media following by engaging with his audience.

Tim is an avid learner and has an amazing talent for educating people. He is a self-proclaimed introvert who feels uncomfortable in large gatherings. But that hasn't stopped him from using search and social media algorithms to gain massive online visibility for his educational podcast conversations with people who have mastered their art.

By late 2022, Tim's podcast, the *Tim Ferriss Show*, surpassed 900 million listeners, making it one of the most popular podcasts in the world. He has also gathered 1.8 million followers on Twitter and 1.1 million on YouTube. I have personally learned a lot from listening to his podcasts. Tim is a true Servant Influencer.

Depending on the field you're in or want to go into, different social network platforms tend to attract and cater to specific skill sets. That's not a hard-and-fast rule. Most people don't limit themselves to a particular network, so there's a lot of overlap among social media. Nevertheless, you can use the field in which you want to learn skills and knowledge as a platform filter.

For example, many specific platforms focus on technical skills. You can create multiple lists of the top places for particular technical knowledge. Still, you can just as easily learn and boost technical skills on broad-based platforms such as LinkedIn, Twitter, Discord, Reddit, or YouTube. These platforms offer ample opportunities for various kinds of learning and support much bigger audiences than specialized technical sites.

If you're interested in building up and sharing business skills, LinkedIn becomes a logical choice, given its heavy focus on careers and management. Like-minded community groups and similarly focused resources can be found in Facebook Groups. You can find business discussions on Twitter and Reddit. Just use your critical faculties to measure the quality of the source material. YouTube has an excellent selection of lectures on various business topics.

In fact, YouTube is an educational platform for almost anything, whether you're switching out a bad car headlight or learning a new song to play on the guitar. Many credible educators on YouTube are sharing their expertise for free. But it is not the only place to learn. Many designers and arts and crafts people who once made their homes on YouTube have built a new audience on Instagram and TikTok. So, those platforms should be on your list if you're looking to learn from or educate makers.

Discord has become a popular hangout for many online course students. Top Udemy instructors have built their own Discord communities, where students can share their journey with their fellow learners.

Growing Your Network

Making Friends on LinkedIn

It's easier to grow a network on LinkedIn than people think. While it's not the only social network on which you can build a following and become an influencer, it works well for most professionals.

LinkedIn supports both Friend and Follower models. When you start building your network, sending connection requests, aka friending, is often the only meaningful way to grow. Here are my step-by-step instructions for making friends on LinkedIn when you don't already have a large network:

- Send connection requests to your real-world friends to get started. They will recognize you and are highly likely to accept your requests.

- Create a profile focused on specific expertise and enable the Creator mode.

- Write high-quality conversation-opener posts about your expert topics.

- Engage with people who comment on your threads, and decide whether or not to connect with them when they are outside your network.

- Analyze the writing structure and emotional hooks in the currently most viral threads and learn the best practices for virality from them.

- Write consistently and frequently over a longer period of time.

To get yourself started on the influencer path, send up to 100 invites a week. That's the limit that LinkedIn allowed in 2022. It may sound like a lot of work, but here's a tip: You don't need to include any kind of greeting with your invite. It's usually better if you don't because people often think you're trying to sell them something if you add a message. If you want, you can add a thoughtful comment on a person's post and then send the invite without a text to make the invite more timely. Chances are a lot of people will accept your invite as simple networking.

Furthermore, you don't just send invites randomly. Send your invites to people who have lots of common friends with you. This focus on network overlap is important in the early phases when you have a small number of connections.

Start targeting thought leaders only after you have an established presence. Before that, they are much less likely to accept your invite. Not all of your invites will be accepted, so delete all the invites that haven't received a response in a few days. You can use this tactic until you hit LinkedIn's maximum connection limit of 30,000.

Normally you will start receiving a steady stream of inbound invites and follows from others way before then.

Once you reach the first 1000 connections, you will begin to have some credibility. To get there faster, you need a high-quality profile. It attracts more inbound invites and improves your conversions on outbound ones. Below, I will show you a three-part strategy for growing your LinkedIn base, including your profile, content, and some "special moves" to boost your presence. First things first–get working on that profile.

Making Friends on Facebook

Facebook has the same friending model as LinkedIn, but they have capped the maximum friend count to 5,000 instead of LinkedIn's 30,000. You can also build an uncapped follower base on Facebook. The best way to network professionally on Facebook is to create a nice profile with work information included, join active Facebook Groups in your industry, and connect with the people who engage with you in the groups.

Some major influencers create a page instead of a profile, but generally, pages are not that useful for building a network. They are mostly meant for businesses and require regular advertising spending for visibility. With a profile, you can join professional groups and build direct relationships. When a person accepts your Facebook friend request, you also gain a direct communication channel with the popular Messenger chat app.

Facebook Groups used to be the best place for professional networking. As the younger demography has moved on and animosity against Facebook has increased, many community admins are looking to move to alternative community platforms. But Facebook can't be completely ignored as it is still the largest social network in the world, with almost 3 billion monthly active users.

Gaining Followers on Twitter and Mastodon

Twitter used to be the place to break the news, with all self-respecting journalists building a presence there. However, over the years, it has become increasingly toxic, with bots, trolls, and Donald Trump dominating much of the conversation. Trump was suspended from Twitter after the Capitol riot on Jan 6th, 2021, resulting in many of his followers moving to other, smaller platforms.

In October 2022, Elon Musk completed the purchase of Twitter for a whopping $44 billion and started rapid-fire changes to make the platform suit his personal tastes and ideologies. This caused chaos and led many people to question the viability of the "public town square of the internet" being owned by an eccentric billionaire. Millions of people, including many journalists, migrated to Mastodon, a decentralized social media platform.

The emergence of Mastodon can potentially change the public perception of how social media should be organized and may lead to social media platforms becoming more interoperable over time.

Twitter and Mastodon both work on the Follower model. Overall, the key to growing your audience on these platforms is to provide valuable and interesting content, engage with your followers, and use the platform's features to your advantage.

So you will need to start by collecting a few followers to make your account credible. But what if you're starting from zero?

The tactics I've seen used over the years for building influence on Twitter include the following:

- Initially, follow a number of your real-world friends and ask them to follow back. That way, your feed won't look completely empty.
- Create a profile focusing on a specific expertise area, and start writing high-quality threads on your topic of choice.

- Engage with people who comment on your threads and maybe follow them.

- Analyze what are currently the most viral threads and learn the best practices for virality from them. Many people have grown audiences on Twitter using an algorithmic approach and simply rehashing trending topics for their own accounts– to great success. Try to create your own mix of content - don't copy verbatim from others without crediting them.

- Act fast on emerging trends since those trends on Twitter have short windows of opportunity. Once something is listed in trending topics, it is already too late.

- At some point, you'll have to use your own take on trending subjects if you want to be seen as credible and authentic. Write consistently and frequently over a period of time.

- When people engage with your threads with comments and in other ways, engage with them so that they feel like you're responsive. If you follow them, they may follow you back. Do this consistently and frequently, and you can build up tens of thousands of followers in a relatively short time frame.

Mastodon is still in its early days of growth, so there are some specific tips for the platform:

- Mastodon is a decentralized platform, so you will have to choose a server to join. Do some research on the best servers with people like you, and join it. This gives you a head start, as the people on the local server are more likely to find and follow you.

- Engage in conversations with people with large followings in your area of interest. This gives you visibility among their circles.

- Use hashtags, as they are the main discovery mechanism on Mastodon.

- Boost posts that you like by reblogging them. Favoriting a toot, Mastodon's equivalent of a tweet, does not increase its visibility, so you are only doing a favor when boosting and commenting.

Making Friends on Discord

If you want to build a professional reputation on this platform, use your real identity. While Discord users are mostly pseudonymous, you can use your real identity here, and it's more common than on Reddit, which expects the users to be anonymous.

Keep in mind that Discord users are predominantly gamers, streamers, and developers. But the network is expanding to new user groups, so you aren't limited to conversations with gamers. Tactics suitable for making friends and building connections on Discord include

- Join active servers in your core expertise area.

- Ask questions and help people with your advice.

- Use the trust built in conversations to get relevant people to connect with you on LinkedIn, WhatsApp, and other platforms.

- When you are ready to build a community, create your own server.

Like Mastodon, Discord uses the structure of servers and groups that can be public or private. Think of servers as communities based on a shared passion or interest. When you begin with Discord, first join active servers within your core expertise area.

Once a member, you can ask questions and help people by giving advice and by answering questions. You can use those conversations to find out users' identities elsewhere. For example, you could ask them for their WhatsApp number or perhaps their LinkedIn profile. You want to do this to turn the Discord group member into a truly professional connection whom you know personally. Consistency across platforms in terms of your professional identity should always be part of your strategy.

By answering questions and providing advice on the Discord servers you frequent, you will start to build some influence in those spaces. You can use that influence by building your own server, which serves as the base from which you build a community around your cause. Again, remember that the Discord demographics skew heavily toward gamers, streamers, and developers. There's also a sizable web3/crypto user base to target if your project is in that space.

Making Friends on Reddit

Reddit's interest-based model takes the form of "subreddits," which are conversations based on specific interests and passions. So as with an interest-based social network, you should join active subreddits relevant to your profession and expertise to start building influence. Once you join, make regular contributions of good quality that the subreddit community will "upvote."

Gaining upvotes is important because it increases your "karma points." Influence and reputation on Reddit can be measured to a large extent by "karma points." Build karma with relevant comments and posts that are upvoted by other users–meaning they found them useful or thoughtful or have some other positive quality. There are some subreddits for which you need a minimum number of karma points to join. To increase your chances of getting upvoted, contribute to a subreddit early in the discussion. Early contributions gain more upvotes than later comments, as the Reddit algorithm keeps the most popular comments at the top.

Quality and utility are also key to upvotes. For example, be explicit and concise if you're answering a question. If you start a subreddit with your own question, search to see whether it's already been asked.

Because you must accept anonymity as the default mode for Reddit, you will face some difficulty building real-world influence that you can transpose to other networks. You could dominate a topic, but that won't give you direct access to the Reddit users who might follow you. Following people on Reddit is always secondary to the topics. Earning a lot of karma might bring personal satisfaction, but nobody will ever know who has all that karma unless you expose your identity. Reddit users aren't there to follow other people but to participate in conversations about subjects that interest them.

Making Friends on YouTube

YouTube leverages both the follower and algorithmic models. Notably, creators on YouTube represent only a tiny fraction of YouTube consumers. That's because you need well-produced, long-form content to succeed. You don't have to produce a movie, but creating your content is more complicated and takes more effort than creating content on other social media networks. All that said, here are some tactics for taking advantage of the network's tools and model to build out your reputation.

- **Create a Channel That's Specific but Not Worn Out**

If you go up against well-known YouTubers in areas of popular interest, you will create a lot of challenges to growing your own presence on YouTube. So focus your channel on specific pop culture that's not broadly covered. Or, create a unique twist on a popular topic or in a common area (but please, nobody needs any more reaction videos). You can also use sports and political events to create timely videos riding the wave of attention surrounding that kind of event. Your goal with any of these approaches is to hack your way out of the oblivion of your channel and gain visibility. Getting the first hundreds and then thousands of followers is hard work.

For example, a number of YouTube creators are producing videos about China to sizable audiences because China is of global interest. Some of these creators use stock footage with commentary about a particular subject, like finance. Think of it as a video podcast. It's a low-cost production because you only have to provide audio and mix it up with some stock videos.

Ask people to subscribe and follow you on all of your videos. As you gain subscribers, you begin building your YouTube followership. If you're fortunate and you get a spike from any of your videos, there's a chance it will take off and gain you followers outside of your subscribers. When that happens, YouTube increases your content visibility for the coming week on the whole channel. And the total views you can gain from that exposure triggers the algorithm to give you more visibility in general.

Building subscribers–by creating a channel that attracts interest and by asking people to subscribe–becomes vital to success on YouTube for one simple reason: it's a network that excels at connecting content with community responses. Although it's not usually thought of this way, video is, by itself, a forum topic. As people respond to the videos you produce and post, they interact with one another in the channel you've built. We should not underestimate the bond that forms between content creators and their audience, as well as the creation and strength of the interactions among the members of the audience. While other networks, notably Facebook, are rich in these interactions, YouTube enables you to build a loyal audience that can become a community through your community live streams.

The subscribers are the foundation on which you make friends and build influence on YouTube. Subscribers follow your work and take part through comments and shares. Every popular influencer on YouTube pays attention to how they communicate with their audience. You should pay attention too.

Livestreams are a powerful way to build a thriving community on YouTube. Imagine broadcasting a live video, and while you're broadcasting, your audience is commenting, asking questions, and you are interacting with them all in real-time. The power of those interactions is more than the ongoing real-time conversation–itself a powerful community builder–but the fact that interacting live helps followers feel like being part of your creative process. When you move outside of the passive viewer paradigm, deeper connections result. You can find an example of how bands will often tease new releases or experiments and let their subscribers in for a sneak peek of an opportunity to see the band jamming or practicing. Some YouTubers have successfully gained paying subscribers through Patreon and other platforms for their YouTube channel to finance and support their work.

Monetizing isn't the same as building a community of influence, although, at the core, they use the same community-building mechanics. This book focuses on making friends and building credibility and influence based on the help and insight you bring to conversations. Your goal from this perspective is to make a positive impact, promote positive change first, and make money as a result.

Making Friends on TikTok

While you can follow people on TikTok, its main networking model is algorithmic. To gain followers, your task is to create content that gets recommended by the algorithm. The difference between TikTok and other social media platforms is that it shows you one video at a time instead of many. This has allowed TikTok to optimize its recommendation algorithm better than anyone else in the industry.

The main algorithmic feed of TikTok is called "For You Page", in short, FYP. Don't expect to see content refined to your tastes right away. The algorithm is very good at learning your preferences once you start interacting with the videos. The beauty of having one video at a time is that TikTok knows exactly what your intentions with each video are. If you skip the video in the middle, it is a sign that it wasn't good for you. Every tap on the visible buttons is a separate signal that personalizes your recommendations.

On TikTok, you won't build influence or following by commenting on others' videos. You need to be a creator and share videos recommended by the For You Page.

The key is to catch the interest of early viewers. What I mean by that is if you can get the first people to see your video to react, that feeds the algorithm, and your video will have some chance to go viral. The number of followers you have initially doesn't matter as much as in follower-based networks. TikTok AI can still make your content viral. Its objective is to show its users engaging content on the platform.

Make short, engaging videos. Unlike the long-form content on YouTube, TikTok videos have to be very short because average view time per total view time drives the video's engagement metric (food for the AI). For example, suppose you post a ten-second video, and people watch it on average for eight seconds. In that case, you will generate the same metric as you would if you had posted a one-minute video and people watched it on average for 48 seconds. It's much easier to grab people's attention and engage them for eight seconds than it is for 48.

While TikTok has become known for short dance videos, there are many more categories that you can target. Don't even bother with a dance video–there are too many to count already, and your likelihood of standing out is low. Instead, you could make a quick and simple how-to guide that lasts less than one minute. How-to guides are an effective TikTok tactic for building a professional reputation. Many content creators have grown their reach fast, producing simple how-to guides. To gain direct followers, think about a personal angle for your videos so people will want to see the next one too.

Boost the depth of responses your video receives to build your reputation. People can respond to your videos with likes and comments. Similar to how you can build a network and community on YouTube, you can post random details about yourself in the comments to generate even more reactions. This tactic will take advantage of the platform's algorithmic boost to magnify your presence.

Also, like YouTube, you can ask people to follow you on every video you make. Ask them in a straightforward, prominent way. TikTok users have grown used to the ask, so give them the opportunity to decide Yes or No. Followership gives you more visibility in those people's For You pages by creating a self-perpetuating loop in which the more people follow you; the more people will be early viewers of your videos. And the more early viewers, the higher the chances that your video will gain virality.

Hashtags are another important way to gain visibility in specific niches. In addition to the For You Page, videos can be discovered from trending hashtags, so you should add a few relevant ones consistently. Finally, you may want to consider the premium Creator account to gain access to better statistics on your performance.

In the next chapter, I will talk about how you can build connections and relationships with people who aren't following or connected with you yet. Helping people is the best way to gain their trust and attention. Being helpful will encourage people to be affiliated with you. That's how you start building your influence in a meaningful way.

3

How to Help People

In the early 2010s, when I was already convinced about behavioral algorithms' negative and positive potential, I set out to build a social address book for iOS and Android. The idea was to build a massive social graph with data from various social media platforms that maps trust between people.

I thought it would be a great idea to help people scale trust and always seek the path of the highest trust when approaching new customers, potential employers, or other opportunities. The actual connection between people would always happen through an introduction by the person with the strongest trust in the person you were being introduced to.

To build a reputation in this market, I decided to become a super-connector by making a lot of introductions. I thought it would help me learn about the challenges people may face when they make introductions.

During the following years, I made hundreds of introductions. I learned how to pitch the value of the introduction to the person I introduced an entrepreneur to. What's more, I learned how to ensure that a meeting between the introduced people happened in a reasonable time frame. This made the introductions valuable and productive for both parties.

I gained a lot of social capital with my introductions. People were genuinely grateful, and I became the go-to person for many successful entrepreneurs when they wanted to connect with others.

The help I offered to people not only built my affinity with movers and shakers in the startup scene. It also helped me grow a powerful network globally. Through my help, I became known not only as an entrepreneur but also as a helpful person.

Face it. When you're just starting to build up your influence, you're just not that interesting to other people. They won't readily accept your connection requests or follow you back. It takes a lot of hard work to become an interesting person in this regard, especially if you're targeting influencers with big networks since they like to network with other influencers. But there lies the opportunity: if influencers want to grow their influence, could you gain their attention by helping them get there?

It works, but not on thought leaders who already have massive followings. It is better to start helping people who are actively building their influence in your space. You don't even have to ask favors in the early phase, as participating in active industry conversations builds your own nascent influence. To make yourself interesting and relevant to other people, build trust by helping them–in any way possible.

If you contribute something to a conversation, offer compelling insight, make an introduction, or perform other helpful actions, people will see that you're a good person. After a while, they start to affiliate with you. Building affinity with rising industry stars is a great way to grow influence - people let you associate with them because you're helping them! This association makes you credible in the eyes of others in the field.

Once you've earned trust by helping people and contributing to their conversations, you can start asking favors. It's okay to ask for favors. People will want to help you if you've helped them first. Robert Caldini labeled this rule of reciprocity as one of the six principles of persuasion. You are building a lot of social capital[24] by helping others.

Reciprocity is very important in community building. You want to give value to the community members first so that they want to reciprocate and provide value to other community members. You can read more about it in Chapter 7.

In this chapter, I talk about how helping others builds trust, affinity, and, ultimately, a community. First, I will explain why you should help first. Then I will describe what kind of help makes you friends. Finally, we will take a look at how this all works on different platforms. Some platforms have tools that make this work easier, and some don't.

Why You Should Help First

If your goal is to build working relationships with the right people (the people you believe can help you in your quest), you must first earn the trust of the people whose circle you want to join. Take the initiative to share your expertise and insights, and experiences. Post useful commentary and point to events that interest these people. Helping people is the easiest way to earn their trust and respect, and helping the rising stars of your industry is good for your own goals.

What Kind of Help Should You Give?

There are three main ways to help on social media: 1) participate in conversations, 2) make introductions, and 3) share positively

---

[24] Social capital refers to the relationships among people who live and work in a particular society. It involves the effective functioning of social groups through interpersonal relationships, a shared sense of identity, a shared understanding, shared norms, shared values, trust, cooperation, and reciprocity (Wikipedia).

about your encounters with others. If you consistently help people in these ways, you can boost your standing and make yourself relevant for those whom you want to add to your network - including the top rising stars in your areas of interest.

Participate in Conversations

Once you have a clear idea of whom you want to add to your network, you're ready to start commenting on their posts and engaging in their conversations. Depending on the platform you are on, you can start by following them. As you become more aware of the conversations they participate in, you can comment on their posts.

Remain consistent and active. After you have commented several times (not just once or twice–you want to appear to them to be someone serious about the area and not a passerby), send them a connection request on LinkedIn. By then, they've acknowledged that you add value to their conversation, so there's no harm in making the invite. Once you get into the circles of big influencers, it's easier to get deeper into their conversations because you have made this reference point to bolster your credibility.

As long as you participate in their conversations on a regular basis, people will think that you're part of their network. Even if you're not well connected at first, they will eventually become part of your network. You can bolster your membership after you've commented three or four times on influencer posts and send them connection requests. They will likely accept your request because you've already helped them so much. Overall, this comment-to-conversation-to-connection path is a low-cost, low-risk way of becoming part of the networks of powerful people without you being a powerful influencer yourself.

Build affinity. During this "getting to know you" phase, affinity builds on itself, and if you have people in the right circles in your friend list, you can leverage that to get more friends in the same circles. Think of it as a friend-of-a-friend-is-a-friend model. To bolster affinity and trust further, look to see if people in the circle are asking for advice or input. That's your opening to offer advice and recommendations and perhaps to recommend some people they should talk to. Make your advice direct and relevant–and offer it when you have something to add, not just to attract attention. As a practice, you should provide advice and recommendations for people who ask for it on their walls.

To move beyond advice and comments, participate in active and productive conversations. You can even try to turn your comments into conversations. After some time, you will become more and more visible on the walls of those you want to affiliate with.

Make Introductions

Participating in conversations sets the ground for making introductions–a simple, effective way to provide value to the people you want to associate with. And by connecting people who can add value to each other, you also gain social capital and build trust, which is essential to becoming an influencer.

Make yourself a connector. Introduce people to each other whom you believe will produce even richer insights and questions. You're already familiar with their ideas and practices from your conversations with them. It's, therefore, inevitable that a lightbulb moment will bring people together in your mind, and you can help others on the network by assisting them in making that same connection.

Tag only those you think will be interested in the conversation or those who can share some insights, advice, and introductions. If you can introduce powerful people to each other, you will certainly boost your standing in the community–even if you're a small player. Just remember not to spam!

Share Positive Experiences

It's not just the positive experience that counts here–you should also speak about your experience in a positive way. When you have a productive call or meeting with a person you respect, and it's not a secret, share some love on social media. Those you meet will feel good about your interaction because they're receiving positive attention. They'll remember you, and the result is that others build affinity with you and the person you met. Places where you meet people, such as conferences, are great for this. You can take a selfie and post it on your social networks, too. Say good things about that person. In a way, you're helping them by sharing your experience and promoting them. And people on your network who know the other person will associate you with this person, further building your credibility.

All of these tactics work toward building your social capital, which is the main support for credibility and affinity–the building blocks of online influence.

How to Help People on Different Platforms

Because different platforms are structured differently, use different models of engagement, and attract different audiences, you'll need to think about how you can help people based on the platform you're operating on. Following are some general principles for popular social media sites.

LinkedIn

The main tool at your disposal on LinkedIn is introductions. By introducing people to one another, you help them build their reputation and trust in your online relationships. Trust is the main ingredient to relationships, both online and in the real world. But it's hard to build online because you're not interacting face-to-face. By making introductions, you can alleviate that obstacle. People will see you as helpful and will likely reciprocate by introducing you, following you, and participating in discussions related to your posts.

- **Introduce People in Your Network**

So how do you make the best use of LinkedIn introductions? What are the most useful tactics you can make use of? For one, make use of LinkedIn group messaging, a common way to build social capital on the network. Say you're in a wall conversation on LinkedIn. In that conversation, someone is asking for help on a particular issue, and you know someone outside the conversation who you believe could help.

You can offer to introduce them by creating a group chat message between you, the person asking for help, and the person you think can help. Now there's an affinity built between them through you–even if they aren't friends yet. You can accomplish all of this within the bounds of the conversation, and it will be seen as relevant and helpful–another link built in a chain of trust.

LinkedIn conversations do have some natural barriers. If you don't establish the value of the introduction, then it can appear random–an unusual occurrence in the messages section. Random remarks can be seen as distractions or, worse, rude interjections. Value arises from the merit the person you invite brings to the conversation and the topicality of the person's comments. In other words, as in many other virtual conversations, value is tied to whether comments match the situation that defines specific parts of the conversation. Introductions that appear random or poorly positioned detract from the trust, damaging the relationships you want to build on your path to influence.

- **Add Value with Thoughtful Comments**

Aside from introductions, practice the ideas of helpfulness and relevance in your own posts. When your comments can be traced to insight and experience, they are more likely to provoke responses. You might receive scores of comments on your comment–an amazing result. Beyond that emotionally satisfying experience, you're building a rich vein of social capital that you can use to extend your network and your fledgling influence.

Your comments can attract influencers to reciprocate by commenting on your posts. If your post gets the attention of a well-regarded influencer in your existing network, the payoff can be massive. The comment is especially valuable if an established influencer leaves it soon after your post went out – early in its lifespan. The comment opens the floodgates to the influencer's followers to see your work, comment on it, and possibly choose to follow you and even endorse you.

- **Tag Relevant People to Help the Author of the Post**

By tagging someone outside the discussion group, you can bring them into the conversation. It's a lightweight way of pulling somebody in, especially if that person adds value by commenting on the ongoing discussion–perhaps with expertise, insight, or a story of their personal experience with whatever issue is being discussed.

Tagging has the same etiquette as introductions. You should not spam people with tags – only pull them in when you see it valuable for both the tagged person and the author of the post.

- **Endorse People You Know**

Endorsements build credibility and social capital on LinkedIn, so you definitely want to work at gathering them and offering them, particularly from and for people you know and whose work you're familiar with.

Please be mindful that many LinkedIn users game skill endorsements and recommendations, so they shouldn't be taken without a grain of salt. On the other hand, some would say that a level of skepticism is already baked into how people view social media. Hence, endorsements and other testimonials are more or less relative in their credibility index.

The healthy and ethical way to view the top endorsed skills on your and others' profiles as signals of aspirations rather than real-life verified abilities.

Introductions, thoughtful comments, tagging extra potential conversation participants, and endorsements are all avenues toward helping people on LinkedIn. In some way or another, these and similar tactics can also be used on other platforms, such as Twitter and the major chat group venues.

Twitter and Mastodon

Compared with LinkedIn, there's much less you can do to help others on Twitter and Mastodon. They are follower-based platforms, and it's much harder to build your network by getting people to follow you if you're not already a known influencer. For example, if you have 50 followers, it doesn't matter how many people you follow. Most of them won't follow you back. That's the dilemma of follower-based platforms, and it's really hard to build your presence unless you bring it with you from other platforms. However, if you want to build more of a presence on Twitter or Mastodon, focus on making high-quality comments and retweet/reblog people who are relevant to your interests and already have a significant following.

If you decide to try, the most effective strategy you can employ is to add extremely high-quality threads and to become famous from those conversations you started. But there's good news: on Twitter and Mastodon, you can participate in conversations and focus on growing that way to start with – you don't have to create the circumstances for building influence all by yourself. Make high-quality conversation contributions. Quality can be measured by relevance coupled with stickiness–an emotional hit or an insightful take on the conversation. There's some chance that your replies are seen as having an equal standing as the original post around which the conversation revolves.

Because the platform is still in its early growth phase, reblogging authors and topics relevant to you on Mastodon can also be helpful as an influence-building tactic. A simple retweet on Twitter doesn't do much; you have to comment or quote a tweet to get noticed. If you add value to the conversation and your take gets some attention, you may gain some affinity with the influencer. You are trying to add value to people in positions of power who have the resources to make a change–whether in the political sphere, the business sphere, or other venues. If any of those people follow you in response, you will accumulate a good amount of social capital that enhances your credibility and visibility.

Weaving other people into your tweets or Mastodon toots can also be effective as a variation. So when you're posting to a conversation, and you've picked up a sharp insight from another poster (perhaps not in the same conversation as you but relevant to the conversation nonetheless), pack their view into your posts with appropriate tagging. Insights can come from anywhere–perhaps you picked up an idea at a conference or a party. Open the current conversation to outside thinkers and observations, no matter the origins of the ideas. If you got exposed to an idea in a conversation with someone outside Twitter or Mastodon, you can still tag them in your post, talk highly of them and why their insight struck a nerve with you, and recommend people to follow them. You are building social capital that can pay out later.

You may even build cross-platform social capital by sharing links to your connections' LinkedIn posts within the Twitter or Mastodon conversations while tagging them to help them grow outside LinkedIn. The tagged person and the local members could perceive that move as helpful, thus enhancing your social capital (and influence).

Community Platforms (Discord, Slack, Telegram, WhatsApp)

Community platforms share similar technologies, so there's no appreciable difference among them, and the same techniques will work on all of them. And the chief thing you have to do on any of them is establish yourself in the group you join. Your first move is to open conversations in groups you participate in and on topics you care about. If you start a conversation, people see that you're an active member of the group.

How do you gain access to the chat rooms you're interested in? Several paths are available to you. For example, if you're participating in or attending a conference, you will often find chat groups associated with the conference. Or you might find a link to a relevant chat group through another social media site. However you find your way in, it's important that right away you set yourself up as an active member who adds value to the group's conversation.

People respond to people, not always to abstract ideas (no matter how impressive an idea it is). To capitalize on connections, tell about personal experiences so that people learn who you are, who you work with, and why you do what you do. The other people in the conversation likely know nothing about you beyond your name, and not even that if you have a pseudonymous identity.

With each personal story, you're building social capital within the group. People begin to identify who you are, and that recognition makes you stand out in the conversation–that's extremely important when you're using a chat group to build influence and to help others build theirs. This is a public secret. Most people don't know how to tell personal stories and don't even think about doing something like it. Yet, it's an easy way to establish yourself as a real player in any chat group conversation. Your personal stories may also prompt others to open up, increasing the affinity and trust of the whole group.

If your conversation proves interesting enough to receive significant attention, be sure to give thanks and credit to those who add value to the conversation. Be generous in your thanks–it makes people feel positive about you, and that's part of the glue of trust and influence. If the conversation starts rolling and there are some valuable contributors with whom you become familiar, connect with them on other social media platforms and participate in their public conversations there.

So, you've started a conversation, it has picked up a little steam, people are reacting to your stories, and you're thanking valuable contributors to keep the momentum moving forward. It's natural that people in the group will combine your actions into an assumption that you're probably some kind of thought leader. As you gain more attention, you also gain scrutiny. As trust between you and your network grows, people may expect you to have certain attributes that they associate with trust. One of those is authenticity, which is the next chapter's subject.

4

How to Be Authentic and Stand Out

In 2017, when the cryptocurrency markets were white hot and a lot of people were hustling for easy money, I was working on a project using blockchain to enable automated incentives for making introductions. At the time, there was a popular meme image going around. It included a guy wearing a shirt made out of gold, a golden necklace, and multiple golden bracelets, saying, "I'm in for the technology." Nobody seemed to believe anyone to be in the crypto industry for any other reason than the prospect of easy money.

But I was a rare exception. I was actually in for the technology. My startup had a real problem to solve with crypto. We were building a global community of people who got paid for making trusted introductions between entrepreneurs and business leaders. The community had grown to 3,000 members in dozens of countries, and we were running into problems making payments. I tried to pay an Indian businessman to introduce a Nordic entrepreneur to a Silicon Valley company executive he knew. Wiring money from Germany to India required complex bureaucracy and was very expensive.

Crypto would enable us to reimburse everyone automatically at next to zero cost. We could make all incentives and rewards programmatic and introduce a slew of micro-payment rewards. We didn't even have to think about currency conversion rates.

We needed to move our trust-based community to crypto–to an ecosystem that tried to minimize trust and in which most large players stayed anonymous. There was only one way to make a move. I jumped in without anonymity, and we built our community as "the most trusted and caring community in crypto."

A lot of people doubted my motives, and I took on many ad hominem smear attacks. There were eight hacking attempts, each more complex than the previous one. But we stayed the course, practicing kindness with everyone and always remaining transparent about everything we did. We had a diverse global team of 27 community admins who loved the culture we were building. It was different and refreshing.

Our community grew from 3,000 to 82,000 members in 182 countries in only a few months. There were many moments when I felt stressed and burned out. But in the end, we gained a tremendous amount of trust, and I met many impact-oriented entrepreneurs in crypto for the right reasons. We even won the Global Blockchain Competition in Singapore in the spring of 2018 with our AI- and blockchain-powered trust graph. Our business grew quickly as a result.

All of that growth and goodwill came out of one simple action: I was authentic, the real me, setting myself and the company up as different in an industry where inauthenticity and pseudonymity were the norms. I didn't try to blend in. I wanted to prove that there was a better way to build blockchain communities. Many people agreed, allowing me to become a trusted industry member.

Up to this point of the book, we have been going over the actions you can take to successfully build influence using social media and how to use that influence to achieve an outcome greater than the one you would get as an isolated individual. In previous chapters, we addressed how to build the basis for online influence and how to choose the best platform to reach your goal. We also covered how to make connections, how to build friendships, and how to start helping people. All those steps will establish you as an active player on the field.

Presenting yourself as authentic is the last step in your preparation.

Being authentic and standing out requires finding a balance between your "brand" - what people know you for and expect from you - and your "personal touch", the empathetic presentation of your brand. When people know what to expect from you, are familiar with your reputation, and can identify you as one of them, trust increases –and trust is the power behind the influence. This is the final step before you can start actively building your influence.

Profile

To attract high-profile professionals and get them to accept your invitations to connect, you should present an engaging, high-quality profile. Why is your profile so important? Because it is your digital business card, establishing you as a credible professional in your field. When done well, you will see an increased conversion of your invites and a faster growth of inbound invites from others.

Let's take LinkedIn as an example. LinkedIn has a robust set of tools for you to use to create an engaging profile and strong personal brand. For example, you can use a few hashtags consistently at the end of your posts. They will help you establish your thought leadership around the chosen topics. People can follow hashtags on the network, allowing you to be visible where it matters.

One of LinkedIn's most important profile features, Creator Mode, is essential for your goal of becoming an influencer and thought leader. Turn that on because it will bring you followers and deepen the relationship with your existing connections. For example, when you enable Creator Mode, people who send a connection request to you will follow you automatically. So you gain more followers even if you don't accept all the connection requests. The Creator Mode also adds a follower count on your profile page, which boosts your social capital and credibility.

These engagements draw from human psychology. People normally check who you are before they send you a connection request or check who you are before they accept your request. While building your presence, you must look credible and interesting, or you will be rejected.

The Creator Mode isn't for everyone. To make it effective, you must create regular content–optimally, two or three posts per week. Continual postings encourage engagement and comments. Be sure to remain authentic–don't invent stories to make yourself look bigger than what you really are or that imply that you know more than you do. People want reality, not a facade. You can augment your credibility as a creator by featuring your best posts, especially those that draw the most attention.

If you're using LinkedIn, pay attention to the About section. By default, this section shows the visitors just the first couple of sentences, and they have to expand to read further. These sentences are essential. People will read more if they are intrigued enough to continue reading, so muster your emotional intelligence to convince the visitor to keep reading. The About space isn't the place to create a fake professional brand—it's a place to show authenticity. For example, you could start with something personal to come across as someone others can relate to. This is often the only chance you have to spur a connection. Finish the About section with a story that augments your profile keywords to reinforce those ideas you want to attract followers for.

If the platform you're using supports it, include a vanity URL. The best strategies are either to mimic the handle you use in other social media accounts, such as on Twitter, or use your full name. Ensure consistency across platforms.

Sharing your contact information depends on your situation. As a business developer or salesperson, you probably benefit from having your contact information clearly visible. If you are a CEO or technical expert, sharing your contact is riskier. We don't live in a world where everybody who reaches out to you is relevant, respectful, helpful, or at least benign. Obviously, people can find you if they try hard enough–but you don't have to roll out the red carpet for the spammers or stalkers.

Those caveats aside, the level of connection you can achieve through your contact information can promote interesting and useful exchanges outside of the social network. For example, I recently received an email from a social psychologist following my LinkedIn account. She was interested in exploring the psychological aspect of AI and algorithmic influence and expressed interest in joining the community I am running. Think about connections you might make beyond any single platform and how they integrate into other aspects of your life.

If the platform you're using has space for listing your top skills, you can make that work for you too. Remember, you're aiming everything in your profile at attracting invitations and followers. So when you list your skills, they don't have to be your present skills. They can be aspirational, a promotional tool to position yourself. Think of them as describing the person you want to become. They speak to who you are and what you want to be good at. You can solicit your connections to testify on your emerging abilities in those areas.

A well-tuned profile is only the first step on your journey to thought leadership on social networks. Your success depends on the content you share and the conversations you participate in.

Give Your Professional Brand a Personal Touch

When you have gathered at least hundreds of followers, you can establish yourself professionally. At the core of that brand is your professional profile–not only in the sense of creating a differentiated profile on social media but also starting to communicate on the topics that you want to be influential in. Combine your character, professional skills, and target audience into a meaningful whole that others will recognize and appreciate.

The core building blocks of an authentic profile are your character, professional skills, and communication style.

- **Personal Character**

When describing yourself, start with your authentic self. Don't build a fake professional facade. I start my profile by describing myself as a husband and father. I start that way because I want people to assess me in terms of my values–that family is important to me. It makes it clear that this is the profile of a specific person, not an avatar behind the screen.

So, as I start with my most important values and then move into the areas of my professional expertise, I create a little bit more authentic connection with the visitors. I tell people what I believe in, and I present a list of keywords that point to my topics of expertise and my target audience. You don't have to do it the same way. You may have personal interests or another way to open your professional profile. What's important is that you present yourself as a real and credible person with integrity. The internet is full of fake profiles, so you build more trust faster by being more human.

- **Professional Skills**

In the following paragraphs, I will refer to LinkedIn since it's the number one platform for professional networking. However, you can adapt the tactics I will illustrate to any social media platform to better fit the platform's underlying model. To note, you don't need to follow these tactics in the order I present them, but if you do, you are sure not to neglect any part of your profile.

First, create a personalized URL within the platform if it allows it. You want people to remember your name and associate it with the connections you are making and the helpful, insightful posts you make, and the introductions you make.

Additionally, include a professional-looking headshot so that people can recognize you and see that there's a real human behind your profile. You can be creative here–matching your headshot with professionally rendered graphic images that evoke emotional appeal or provoke curiosity.

If the platform supports a headline, include in yours what you think are the most relevant keywords. In my case, I use keywords that I want people to use to discover me. For example, if someone searches for "impact or community," they will find me because that idea appears in my headline. I am often approached by people who find me because of the term I use in my headline. Further, on LinkedIn specifically, you can customize hashtag settings to clue people into the topics you often discuss in your posts.

Separate from hashtags and keywords, you can showcase your top skills and ask people to endorse you for those skills on LinkedIn. As I mentioned before, skill endorsements have already been gamed on LinkedIn. Therefore, the most useful way to think about them is not to look back but look ahead to what you want to become. Past projects are showcased as a part of your work history, so consider the skills section as a way to show your future. By describing aspirational skills, you define your future goals to the broader public.

Beyond a broad public audience, your aspirations also identify you to your target audience. They signal your intention. In that way, your list clarifies what kind of people would like to connect and communicate with you. True, your aspirations aren't voted on, as are your project profile and the skills it displays. But that doesn't mean people won't grant you some face credibility for your intentions. Put yourself out there. In my case, I listed emotional intelligence, artificial intelligence, and big data. These are the skills I'm most actively developing, so they can be why people connect to me.

- **Talk Like a Human**

Personalizing and professionalizing your profile affects how others perceive you, especially regarding the credibility they will grant you. To deepen that connection, work on your personal communication style. Your style should be authentic. It should be a style that people recognize and can empathize with, so they know it's not a bot behind the words. And, as I've said before, it should be helpful, insightful, and carry an emotional hook

Why all the attention to communication style? Simple: Text-generating AIs can flood public walls and blogs with SEO-optimized content that uses all the right keywords. You have no chance against that tsunami of content. Therefore, you must use your biggest asset, which is that you are human. People want to talk to other people, and they crave personal, emotionally connecting stories.

> In November 2022, OpenAI released the latest application of their large language model GPT, called ChatGPT. A massive wave of hype followed it as people discovered that it could do almost anything you can imagine: creatively write anything from poems to jokes to theatrical acts, create strategies, explain philosophies, generate and document software modules.
>
> Many felt that we entered a new era where an AI assistant can dramatically increase the productivity of almost any professional. Some were worried that our societies might be unable to adapt to such a rapid change.
>
> One thing is certain – text written by human writers will become an ever-shrinking portion of texts available online.

- **Find Your Communication Style**

Earlier in this book, I talked about why it's best to tell relatable, emotionally connecting stories. That's what people respond to. It's a requirement for thought leadership because to achieve that station, you have to engage people by sparking conversations as well as actively participating in them. Is your style simple, useful, funny, sophisticated, controversial, emotion-sparking, or something else? What is natural to you? What approach would work with your target audience?

If answering these questions is difficult, think instead of the content you find engaging. Perhaps it's something like TED talks, where insight or unexpected ideas can emerge from research and personal experience. Maybe it's content that spurs you to debate or makes you pause to consider your own position on an issue. Perhaps it's fiction or some other published work that stirs your emotions.

You don't have to be a creative writer, professional speaker, or renowned researcher speaker to develop and practice your communication style. You have everything you need–you're human, you can draw on experience, think about the future, and talk about all of it clearly and simply so that others can understand and relate.

- **Language Matters**

Language plays a critical role in your communication and as part of your professional brand. The language you use defines the audience you target. If you are based in a country with a dominant local language, for example, and that is your core target group, you should use that language.

If you target international audiences or want to build a global professional community, the best choice is to go with English. Over history, global language standards have changed. Right now, English is the coin of the realm. In the future, it may be some other language. That said, if you've built an audience in one language, you will lose most viewers when you switch to another language. So a wide-based language, or even a global one, can help you reach and maintain the largest audience possible.

On social media, you can see that members of separate filter bubbles develop their own language. That happens in all kinds of circumstances, as a matter of fact. Academic journals of different disciplines use jargon as a shortcut to complex ideas and to identify the writer and the reader as members of a specific community. An online example is the popular Reddit forum r/WallStreetBets, which has millions of members who have a distinct way of communicating with each other. Terms and phrases like "diamond/paper hands," "apes strong together," "hedgies, "muties," and "tendies" help group members identify with the group and prevent outsiders from easily entering the conversation–at least until they have some skill at the language.

A communication secret that lies at the heart of social media bubbles is that once you grasp the jargon and the character of the group's communication, you can blend in with them. This isn't simply a voyeuristic or a surveillance tactic. Remember–you're trying to build an audience. One way you can do that is to use your ability to communicate within different bubbles, cross those bubbles, and get members from each bubble to engage with your content as a single audience.

It's easy to assume that different groups have polarizing views and approaches. However, if you communicate at a level higher than that of the group and you bring members of different groups into the conversation, those audience members have the opportunity to interact with one another in areas outside of their ingroups. Your conversation can operate as a middle ground, a safe space for open exchanges. It's up to your audience members if they can muster the curiosity and courage to interact outside of their ingroup, but you can at least provide the ground on which it's possible. That's the start of influence that makes a real impact.

In the next chapter, I will discuss and share my lessons of experience in how you start the actual influencing of people now that you've identified where you want to influence, whom you want to influence, and how you relate to your audience in an authentic, credible way. Some areas that we will look at include setting the right goals for your influence, working with the social media platform you want to use and ride their AI waves, and using your newly gained superpower responsibly.

5

How to Influence People

Even though I have worked on behavioral algorithms since 2007, I first started experimenting with social media influencing in 2016. My first viral social media post was an answer I wrote to a question on the small, at the time, social Q&A platform Quora. It got over 360,000 views and over 8,700 upvotes. The answer was about my life philosophy: we shouldn't get stuck in repeating routines but rather add new experiences to our daily lives and appreciate small things like a child.

The glowing comments were like an avalanche.

"This is possibly the most enlightening answer I have ever read on Quora. I'm speechless."

"Wow…..you changed me for good!"

"I love this - thank you for opening my eyes and seeing a whole different perspective in life!"

As the love poured in, I started realizing the true power of social media in making a positive impact. You can literally change lives by sharing your ideas and wisdom. If you are an influencer, it is up to you if this is for the better or, the worse.

I made the post on Quora at a time when I was reflecting on my fatherhood. My oldest son had just graduated high school at 17, and I realized the two others would graduate a few years later, making the most important job of my life come to an end. I was 20 years into my professional life and wanted to make sure I'd spend the next 20 years wisely and on a good cause, knowing I didn't have any daily responsibilities at home anymore.

The success of my reflections sparked me to start experimenting with building personal influence through my knowledge of social media algorithms, proving that it was possible to spark healthy conversations in the age of general toxicity. First, I started growing my LinkedIn network to enable a larger reach. I shared the learnings from that journey in Chapter 2. Then, I started commenting on other people's conversations and joining industry groups to help and learn from others. I shared some of the learnings in Chapter 3 and built the base learnings for Chapter 7. By the summer of 2017, I had become an influencer and consistently gained over a million monthly views to my LinkedIn posts.

Influence is the power to affect others. If you influence someone, you change that person's beliefs, thinking, or action in an indirect but important way. While influence has been discussed since Aristotle (and universally across cultures and time), its nature and practice are different now in the age of artificial intelligence.

With people spending up to 12 hours a day online, there is only one scalable way to influence people today—digitally. Your ability to influence others depends on how much they see you online, which depends on the algorithmic feeds of major social media platforms.

That means you need a plan unless you want your influence to be passively controlled by an AI. In building out your plan, consider how to set your goals for your influence, leverage the different platforms and ride the waves of their particular algorithms, and use your newfound, powerful influence responsibly. A well-designed plan will set you up to turn your influence into opportunities of all kinds.

Earned vs. Manufactured Influence

During the era of broadcast media, you could only become influential by being extremely good at something. This is what I call *earned influence*.

Top politicians, athletes, entertainers, successful entrepreneurs, as well as award-winning artists and scientists, earned influence via interviews in broadcast channels and printed media.

Social media has fragmented our attention. Instead of a few curated broadcast channels, every one of us has an algorithmically filtered, personalized feed in various social media channels.

This has launched a new kind of influence that is open to everyone. If you can game the algorithms, you don't have to be the best expert or performer in anything. There are now scores of YouTubers, Instagrammers, TikTokkers, and other social media personalities who have become influencers simply because of their ability to make their content viral.

These people are famous for being famous. They have risen to influence because of their ability to hack distribution algorithms and content to be more visible on social media than other users. This is what I call *manufactured influence*.

Tactics for Winning Views

We learned in Chapter 4 that authenticity and credibility form the foundations for influence. The way you present yourself–your professional profile or brand–is the front door to your thought leadership.

You continue that authentic presentation in every post you publish. In that context, images play an important role. In 2017, the LinkedIn algorithm favored text-based content to imagery, prompting growth hackers to use emojis to bring at least some visual appeal to the text. Now that has changed, and images are ubiquitous.

The right kind of images helps people discover your content if the platform you've picked supports them. Selfies, especially with other people in professional settings, are generally interesting. Recognizable celebrities are also great attention grabbers. Stay far away from old-school stock photos–pretty much anything else is a huge improvement. People respond to people, so landscapes and nature scenes don't connect as strongly to them as pictures of other humans.

That still leaves plenty of room for creativity and even humor in your posts. For example, you can try funny Venn diagrams or other professional meme imagery. If you use quotes from a famous person, check your sources. Not everything was said by Albert Einstein or Mark Twain. Or Steve Jobs or Elon Musk, for that matter. Keep in mind that when you match a quote with a picture of someone, people will attribute the quote to the person in the image. Pro tip: Don't stick a quote on a picture of you. Visitors will see that as egotistical.

Make your text mobile-friendly. Write only one or two sentences per paragraph. Longer paragraphs are hard to read on mobile, and people will bail out of the post in the middle. The vast majority of the views that you get will come from mobile users. The regular paragraphs you write on your laptop might look fine, but visitors to your feed will see a long, difficult slog on mobile.

To achieve mobile-friendly text, follow these simple instructions: After every second sentence, skip the next line and start a new paragraph. It may look weird to you on the desktop, but it looks amazing on mobile. Optimizing your text for mobile will rack up more views than it would have in a longer form.

Tell stories in the form of the hero's journey. In narratology and comparative mythology, the hero's journey, or the monomyth, is the common template of stories that involve a hero who goes on an adventure, is victorious in a decisive crisis and comes home changed or transformed. Think of *The Hunger Games, Shrek, The Wizard of Oz*, and the travels of Marco Polo or Ibn Battuta.

The American author Joan Didion once wrote that we tell stories to live. But we don't need reasons to tell stories–the need to tell them and hear them is deep within us. Writing in the form of the hero's journey doesn't require you to be Homer or "even" Joan Didion. Dave Schools followed this well-honed model to create a single post that was viewed almost 2 million times.

In School's analysis, there are three must-haves: 1) Present a dire problem; 2) Present practical takeaways–something relatable and inspiring; 3) End with a thought-provoking question and a challenge. That formula worked for Schools, and it has worked for many, many others.

Before you write a story of your struggle through big trouble and your eventual emergence as a winner, understand that many influencers have used similar storylines in their posts (because the form is so natural to us). But here lies a depressing fact: many of the stories they tell aren't real. If an influencer tells a hero's journey about themselves, it rarely has happened to them. They tell those stories because they know that it keeps people returning to their posts.

That's one of the sad parts of the race to game algorithms. People know these stories work, so they create fake stories to get views and influencer status. This also applies to many sob stories on LinkedIn, which are there simply for the views, not for their truth value.

Always ask one or more questions at the end of your post to spark a conversation. A well-crafted question attracts comments, and comments drive traffic more strongly than reactions. Ask people to connect or follow. This small tactic reduces the psychological friction people can feel sending connection requests. If you ask, you'll get many more inbound requests and grow your followers faster.

The more comments you receive, the more traffic you generate. Do you want to spark higher-quality conversations? Make sure the first sentence in your post draws attention. In a LinkedIn feed, for example, readers usually only see the first sentence and then have to expand to see more. If the first sentence isn't inviting, viewers won't expand your post and, as a result, won't engage with your conversation either. How does the platform you're using present these "invitations?"

If you publish a text without an image, you can still use simple emojis. Use them in the first sentence to boost the chances a reader will expand your post. I often use 👇 emoji in my headlines to prompt users to open for more.

One more point: use your chosen hashtags consistently to gain your thought leadership within the right keywords.

Who and When Matters

Creating traction with your posts during the first hour greatly affects the amount of social proof, authenticity, and credibility you can build online. Share your post at a time when your followers are online and can engage. If you're curious about whether you're gaining attention, you can often predict the total views from early numbers. For example, you have to gain thousands of views during the first hour to have a chance to reach 100,000+ total views. Don't try to resuscitate your post if you don't gain that kind of momentum during the first hour. Its time has passed.

Timely comments from people with huge followings are pure gold for your posts. In the past, people often tagged known influencers in posts in the hopes that they would comment. That custom has died down somewhat because platforms like LinkedIn started penalizing tag spamming, whether it was the use of hashtags or people tags.

In the past, if you included external links in your posts, then you might be penalized, which would hamper your visibility. LinkedIn, for example, didn't want to send people out of the platform. But users ignored the "rule" and started to post links in the comments. LinkedIn was forced to change the algorithm to reduce the penalty for external links. To keep people in, they added a warning to all outbound links to create a barrier to exit. If part of your strategy is to generate traffic to your website, barriers like that make LinkedIn and other platforms that operate similarly less than ideal for funneling traffic to your business or any other web-based entity.

Using social media management tools to share on multiple networks is fine. But don't use bots or other tricks to automate your posts and responses. Some social networks will suspend your account for that practice or even ban you for good.

Special Moves You Can Make

All users want to hit on a post that goes viral. If it happens to a post of yours, then let it fly. Don't post new entries immediately afterward, thinking you can multiply your chances of going viral. You're more likely to slow down the viral energy surrounding the original post by splitting the visibility among several posts. Rather, keep conversing in the one that is flying!

Have you ever wanted to feel the excitement of seeing your content go viral? Just how can you increase its chances? I've done it many, many times in experiments, and it's always fun. Based on what I've learned, here are some special moves you can use to create a viral post.

Mix topical interest and go cross-platform with it. For example, pick an emerging viral trend from Twitter, and join it early on LinkedIn. I call this "riding the wave." To get the best results, you must get on the trend bandwagon a little before everyone else starts sharing it. This won't help you build focused thought leadership, but it does help you make big numbers and gain many new followers quickly.

Finally, you gain followers by using language specific to a certain filter bubble to target it. Want to target Reddit's r/wallstreetbets investor army? Use words like "ape", "diamond hands", and other in-group terms, and they will recognize you as "one of our own."

Add language that targets opposing bubbles to pull in a broader audience and energize the comments section. But plan carefully because the discussion may get out of control.

> **Emoji Reactions, the Viral Enabler**
>
> In October 2015, Facebook announced the release of the emoji reactions. Mark Zuckerberg explained that they were there to help you better understand how your friends felt about your post. But there was another reason that he didn't mention.
>
> Facebook wanted to know why specific types of content go viral. It was already widely known that emotional reactions gave a lift to the content shared on social media. Therefore, Facebook reasoned that if platforms could measure that reaction, they could quickly understand why a particular piece of content spread so fast.
>
> On the surface, emojis were harmless little cartoons that let users quickly express their feelings about the content they interact with. But underneath, they were a mechanism for Facebook to understand which emotions carried the virality of any piece of content.

Set Goals for Your Influence

Setting influence goals isn't simply a matter of "what I want people to do" plus "how I get them to do it." If it were, humans wouldn't have spent centuries perfecting different techniques. (And we're still working on it.) You will need to examine multiple considerations when you set goals for your online influence.

When it comes to influencing, bigger is not always better. Sometimes it is better to engage a small but powerful group of thought leaders in an intimate setting. Are you trying to reach a particular audience or a part of that audience? Or are you trying to reach a broader audience that extends across filter bubbles? Think of the political spectrum, for example, or how even nonpolitical partisan ideologies and worldviews differ and often don't connect to one another except in opposition.

Do you want to reach a niche audience or a broad audience? That's different from filter bubbles because audiences often divide among interests rather than antagonistic positions. Do you want to create a broad, if shallow, impact on a large audience, or do you want to make a deep and lasting impact on a small group? Do you intend your impact to be short-lived but intense to affect a specific decision? Or do you intend for your influence to last longer and be part of how your audience makes decisions?

Partisan or Bubble Bursting?

This critical choice will exert great power over your influence online. Critical because, usually, whichever path you choose, it's really difficult to go back to the other. In fact, if you try to change your focus at some point, you're likely to alienate your initial audience. Typically, when you concentrate on a portion of society rather than make your discussion more general, audience growth is much faster.

- **Partisan**

Building influence within a partisan community avoids many difficulties because the audience is more homogeneous. To borrow liberally from Aristotle, it's easy to praise Athenians when you're in Athens. In a partisan group, there's less friction among the audience members because they all agree with you and each other to a large extent. People love to find like-minded people who talk to them about familiar ideas seen from a familiar perspective. It's comfortable and reassuring. Conversations with the groups and their members are easier.

It's easy to think of partisanship as political, but people form and are loyal to many other kinds of groups. For example, vegetarians set themselves apart from omnivores. Vegetarians adopt their diet for any number of reasons: religious practice, environmental reasons, animal welfare, and so on. Likewise, there are people who are fully in the camp of crypto and its promises of a decentralized financial system free from the machinations of governments. There are others who value the stability of national currencies and international monetary policy in creating order in financial markets. If you're working toward building influence, expand your idea of partisanship to include homogenous groups bound by common ideals and interests rather than groups bound by tribalism and opposing other groups.

The advantage of speaking as part of a homogeneous group is that it's much easier to grow an audience for your thought leadership. Human nature is to group with and listen to other people like us. Oftentimes influencers who do not mind being in one camp or another–whatever their genuine attitude–just take a side because it helps them build clout. In brief, the upsides to influencing a partisan group include:

- Your audience is easier to grow and manage.

- You're speaking to the choir, so there is less friction between you and the members

- Group members get along well, so conversations are easy to start and continue.

But the drawback of the partisan approach, and it's a sizable one, is that it limits your future options. Group members tend to exhibit what psychologists call *confirmation bias*. The self-affirmation and support found in the group make it difficult to entertain outside ideas and perspectives. If you choose to build your influence within a partisan group, it's hard to change sides or even to become a generalist. People will remember you as supporting one side or another and will likely dismiss your conversations or remain suspicious of your intentions. You won't have much influence with an audience like that. Long-term repercussions should play a large role in your decision to build influence among a partisan or a general audience.

- **Bubble Bursting**

Building a non-partisan, bubble-bursting audience is a lot harder than building a partisan one, but working across filter bubbles can free your future options should you change your focus to something more particular. But don't limit yourself to the idea that it's either one or another. You can be partisan and bubble-bursting at the same time.

Granted, crossing partisan boundaries makes influence-building efforts much more difficult. Perhaps it's important to you to speak to a diverse audience because you want to focus on commonalities, "what unites us," rather than differences, "what separates us". For example, someone could follow an influencer talking about electric cars as a climate activist or performance car lover. They might have opposing views on climate change, but the love for electric vehicles might unite them.

The bubble-bursting approach creates opportunities for conversations to turn ugly. You must muster considerable empathy and patience to manage such a group. From the start, you will need to care when opening conversations between different groups, especially those with opposing worldviews. You definitely don't want to create the kind of social friction that can devolve into a fight.

That careful curation may be worth it to you because you want to build a bigger, more diverse audience for your ideas, your products, or whatever else you want to present. You can build a network of friends or an audience of followers, drawing people from all different bubbles. But it is much more complex because you can't pick a side and run–you will have to be interesting without triggering a segment of your network to leave.

If you succeed, you can launch conversations about timely subjects, and your audience will naturally generate secondary topics that power the conversation forward.

So taking the pluses and minuses, setting a bubble-bursting intent for your influence:

- enables a bigger audience
- requires a lot of skill to manage
- demands careful monitoring so that conversations don't turn ugly
- keeps your future options open in terms of targeting or building audiences to influence

General or Niche Audience

Niche audiences are not the same thing as partisan ones. When you think of general versus niche, think about the level of expertise needed to understand the message you are sharing. You need to have a simple idea with a general appeal to general audiences. You can be much more specific for niche audiences and expect a certain level of expertise in the target audience.

- **General Audience**

The membership of general audiences is necessarily diverse. But there's at least one strong enough common interest that unites an audience's members. Members of one ideology, for example, might prefer to approach a problem like climate change in terms of the vehicles they buy, the personal environmental choices they make, and so on. Members of a different ideology might not consider those acts as important or simply not believe there is any reason to make decisions about vehicle purchases other than personal choice. And yet members of both camps will buy vehicles–their transportation needs are common to each.

General audiences offer some advantages to influencers. For example, because differences are secondary to commonly held needs, you can more easily create conversations that rich a broad selection of people in reach. A general audience responds only to simple enough messages. That's what makes memes powerful.

One contemporary example: in late February 2022, The United States offered to evacuate Ukrainian President Volodymyr Zelensky from Kyiv, the capital of Ukraine, which was being attacked by Russia. Reportedly, he responded, "I need ammunition, not a ride." This was a simple and powerful message that let everyone know that Zelensky is not giving up, motivating Ukrainians to follow their president to do their absolute best to defend their country. It also unified western governments to provide military support for Ukraine.

There are always considerations to account for when you're communicating with general audiences. For one, because you must keep your conversations simple and entertaining for your audience, professionals might dismiss you as a lightweight, not an in-depth expert–not exactly good for your professional influence.

The answer to those dismissive reactions is to mix in enough professional content to establish a proper level of thought leadership. Even if members of the general audience won't understand all of your more professional content and will ignore reacting to it, they may still get the positive idea that you know what you are talking about. This leaves room for influencers to talk about a wide variety of topics from a wide array of perspectives and to argue from a range of possibilities.

One caveat to the ease of building a general audience is that, usually, you will need to bring in some social capital from outside the group. In other words, it helps if you arrive with credibility from some other area, perhaps being a celebrity, author, or athlete. Otherwise, it can be hard to get the attention of a general audience because they have no previous experience with your identity.

Another feature of general audiences, which I discuss in more detail below, is that your impact on a general audience will be typically shallower and shorter-lived than it would be for a niche audience. That's simply a matter of social dynamics. General audiences have broad tastes and needs. They also move from one topical area to another–sometimes rapidly. So in sum, things you need to weigh when you are considering general audiences include:

- the potential of bigger, broader total reach
- the potential of bigger, broader business, social, and intellectual opportunities
- the need to share broadly appealing and simple topics
- the fact that it's harder to win attention and gain a following vs. focusing on a niche audience
- the fact that it usually requires major success noted by mainstream media first
- **Niche Audience**

Like partisan audiences, it's easier to build up a niche audience than a general one. The tastes and interests of niche audiences are more uniform than a general audience. A niche audience's attention to your conversation will be keener, so conversations tend to be more dynamic and self-perpetuating. If you have your own products or services to sell or cause you to want to champion, a niche audience is typically easier to monetize than a general audience.

Unlike a general audience, a niche audience is a more fertile ground on which you can become a thought leader. Conversations are more focused, and as a participant and instigator of conversations, you are more likely to appear as an expert. That gives you the license to talk about more expert topics and steer away from vague general topics that don't spark profound responses.

Together with a willingness to engage in conversations as a knowledge-sharing activity, a niche audience allows you to make a deeper impact on the people you influence. They are already predisposed to ideas within the boundaries of interests that define the niche. And so, introducing new ideas, new perspectives, and solutions can find more ready and willing sets of ears. Likewise, niche audiences are more prone to go deeper into a subject than general audiences.

Taken together, the salient points of practicing influence with a niche audience include:

- easier to build and monetize
- offers the possibility of becoming a thought leader
- offers the possibility to talk about more expert topics
- potentially deeper impact on those who are influenced

Shallow Impact on Many or Deep Impact on a Few?

Closely related to the differences between general and niche audiences is the difference between shallow and deep impact. It's readily apparent that the impact of your influence would tend to be shallow the larger and more diverse your audience. And your influence would be deeper or more profound if you addressed a niche audience. In short, there's an inverse relationship between the depth of your impact and the profile of your audience as general or niche.

- **Shallow Impact: Short-Term and Transactional**

The audience size tends to disperse your impact, much like a stone dropped into a lake has less impact than one dropped into a sink full of water. That's not to say you can't achieve results through a shallow impact. A world-famous pop star may have a shallow impact, reaching audiences who buy the star's music or attend the shows, for example, but aren't close to other fans or to the artist. Nevertheless, the star's art can create a loyal fanbase whose members are united in their appreciation and passion, making a much deeper impact on them. Think again of Zelensky's response: on the one hand, it is simple and short, but it also strikes a deep chord, making a profound impact.

If your goal is more short-term and transactional, a shallow but broad impact is a good choice. For example, suppose you focus the impact of your influence on persuading people to purchase a product or service, donate to a charitable cause, or vote for one political candidate over another. In that case, you're better off reaching more people, and your argument doesn't have to be deep enough to change behavior but only enough to encourage one choice over another. A key feature of this kind of shallow impact is that it's often practiced at one moment in time–it's keyed to a single decision, not a long-term commitment.

With shallow impact, you look to gain the broadest possible reach -which is why it's so closely related to general audiences. For transactional decisions, that's exactly where your influences will play most effectively. It's hard to win this game–just think about how much money and effort companies devote to marketing their products and services. Winning usually requires a broad appeal. And winning (i.e. successfully influencing others) is often a field of a few big hits and multiple misses. But that's to your advantage in this situation. Because of the short-term focus of your influence on a general market, the ramifications of your effort that is off target or unsuccessful are small–the audience quickly moves to the next thing grabbing their attention. Unless your failure is big, which may end your chances of trying other approaches immediately after.

To sum up, you may want to focus on a shallow impact if you want people to make one-time decisions, such as:

- purchasing a product or service
- donating to your cause
- voting
- **Deep Impact: Long-Term Commitment**

Your influence will tend to run deeper if you address a small, more homogeneous audience. Whatever your end goal is for influencing this audience, it starts with building a relationship. And for relationships to form and sustain themselves, they need deep connections.

Along with running more deeply, an impact such as this asks for a long-term commitment rather than a transaction. If your goal is to persuade people to change perspectives, to believe in a just cause, or to sacrifice for a greater good, only a deep impact will help you achieve those ends. It's possible that within a general audience, you can build commitment through a long series of transactions–marketers call this brand loyalty–but it's the kind of commitment that eases a transaction, not one that changes beliefs.

Deep impact is also an effective path toward thought leadership, as group members can more easily separate your insights from the hubbub of social dynamics. Think of it as scanning for a radio signal while driving your car–the strong signal from a large commercial station (deep impact and connection) scans more easily than a smaller college-run station. The influence that makes a deep impact creates alliances and relationships, and without those commitments, your influence will flounder.

Whether you're fostering thought leadership to deepen an allegiance to a product or a position, conjuring thought leadership to enhance your career or your standing in a field of interest, or working to advance interest in a cause, a deep impact can move people in your audience to:

- become an advocate for a cause
- become an active community member
- permanently change behavior or worldview
- support or acquire a company

Leverage Your Platforms and Ride Waves

To move into a position of influencing people, you must create and share interesting content. In the past, the path to winning the content game was to be a good writer. This is rapidly changing now that text-generating AIs like OpenAI's GPT are broadly available. There is a non-zero risk that public social media walls become so infested with AI-generated content that the whole industry will have to change the way content is discovered and engaged with.

But let's set all that aside for the moment. Are there any future-proof ways to create content that leads to thought leadership? Yes. It is all about sparking conversations. People like to engage in conversations–it practically defines what it is to *be* human.

Conversations are valuable forms of engagement on all social media platforms. If you are the regular conversation starter in your area of expertise, you are also the de-facto thought leader. So how can you become a good conversation starter?

Let's start with the basics. And don't worry that you're starting from scratch. You'll have time, even if you're just starting, to build up your conversational skills. You won't lose viewers simply by not having engagement in your early conversation openers.

How to Draw Attention

Make sure the first sentence stands out. People decide if they want to read your post based on the first 1-2 sentences. Many social networks don't show the full post at once, so the viewer must be convinced to read further.

Use visuals like images, videos, and emojis because they draw attention better than text. Think carefully about what kind of visual you use to get people interested and how to spark a conversation from there. Stock photos are not a good shortcut.

Write in a mobile-friendly way with chapter spacing after every couple of sentences. People will not read to the end. Short paragraphs might look odd on a desktop, but it doesn't matter. Most of your content will be discovered and consumed on mobile devices.

How to Tell a Story That Resonates

Previously, I told you about the power of the "hero's journey" story. That's a template of stories that involve a hero who goes on an adventure, is victorious in a decisive crisis and comes home changed or transformed.

Whether you call it a hero's journey or something else, it's important that the stories you tell connect emotionally. People are more likely to engage with emotionally connecting stories and remember them much longer. I'm sure you remember a favorite moment from your childhood and could tell a story about it. Even if you've forgotten the rules of factoring you learned in math class when you were a kid.

Apply this approach to tell stories about your business, cause, or career, and you should see your audience grow much faster.

How to Leverage Social Proof

When people react, comment on, and reshare your posts, they are writing. Timely comments from relevant influencers have an outsized impact on the visibility of your content. When an influencer participates, the feed algorithms share the content with many followers. The fact that an established influencer joins your conversations creates the social proof that acts as a "seal of approval," lowering the resistance others might feel toward interacting with a stranger.

By consistently starting and participating in social media conversations and by making your contributions valuable–not just making remarks or likes–you gain more opportunities to generate social proof. That proof can improve your visibility and grow your number of followers. It can even form a virtuous cycle in which your growing visibility and audience attract industry leaders and other kinds of influential people, which in turn provides more social proof and increases your influence. It brings attention to your goals, whether it's a cause you advocate, the career you're advancing, or an innovation for which you're trying to build support.

With social proof, you gain the benefit of others seeing you as one of the influential leaders in your chosen subject area. People will trust you faster, and you can build relationships easier when you gain that status.

As important as social proof is, getting people to talk about the ideas and subjects of the conversations you start can't be ignored. So you need to spark the conversation through a question or by telling a story so that it resonates with others. In the conversations you start, you want people to share their own versions of the same story or feel part of the conversation.

How to Spark a Conversation

Ask questions at the end of your posts to spark conversation. A well-crafted question attracts comments, and comments drive traffic more reliably than a bunch of "likes."

Actively participate in the conversations you and other industry influencers start. Always try to increase the quality of the conversation and to grow recognition of your thought leadership.

Ask people to connect or follow at the end of your posts or threads to accelerate the growth of your audience.

How to Ride a Wave

Traction during the first 1-2 hours matters. That is why you want to share the post at a time when your followers are online and can engage.

Pick an emerging trend from Twitter, join it early, and ride it. This won't help you build focused thought leadership, but it does help you make big numbers and gain a lot of new followers quickly.

When you have a winning post with a lot of traction, focus on keeping the conversation going and wait before pushing out the next opening.

Use Your Influence Superpower Responsibly

Here's a slight variation to the golden rule: Influence others as you would like others to influence you. Influence, especially when practiced at the highest levels, is the ability to shape other people's opinions and behavior. If you can develop that ability, you must deal with the ethical questions that come with it. As with so many areas of life, consequences don't arise from the talent and skill you've developed but from your practice of them. Not everyone is concerned with the ethical dimensions of influence, but I believe that if your goal is to create audiences and to develop the skill to influence those audiences toward some end, you ought to behave as a good human being while you're at it.

Of course, people debate about what makes a "good human being." All sorts of equations have been developed to answer this vexing question. Amid those philosophical quandaries, I want to argue for a simple, commonsense approach. There's a reason the golden rule is golden; we assign it the rarest of values. Rare but obtainable.

Meeting this standard is harder than ever in our hyper-connected world with its anonymity and with the algorithms that encourage attention-getting over help-giving. So at the very least, as you develop influence that reaches bigger audiences and you deepen connections that enable you to shift the beliefs and perspectives of others, be aware of the possible unintended consequences.

You can't get around it—your increased visibility will also increase the number of haters who want to pick and complain and ridicule–that's their strategy for gaining visibility. Don't worry about it. You can't please everyone. You shouldn't even try. Not if you want to remain authentic. The more you talk in public, the higher the risk that something you say backfires spectacularly. You may become a target of a cancel mob without even understanding why random people take time to attack you. But if you strive to leave the world a better place than you received it, you'll be able to practice influence that helps people and encourages them to do the same. No hater will achieve that.

Your notion of what is good for people is surely different from other people's notions. We don't all have to think the same. We can't, anyway. As you practice influence, you must let people make their own decisions. You're not responsible for their reactions to your influence, but influence in good faith, and chances are your efforts will be reciprocated.

These are lofty aims. They may be more than you want to shoot for. Perhaps you only want to sign people up for a cause or increase sales of your company's products and services. Nothing wrong with that. But no matter what level of influence you wield, you can practice in a way that makes positive change possible. The product you tout can solve real problems. The cause you champion can make lives better. And your influence can be a responsible superpower that others will recognize and want to join with.

In the next chapter, I will turn toward the next stage of influence you can work on. In that effort, you will learn how public conversations build thought leadership while private conversations build relationships and trust–both essential to developing new opportunities.

Those opportunities may operate for your own good: to enhance and accelerate your career, for example. Or they may operate in a larger sphere: growing your business, for example. You need both, and understanding the difference separates authentic influence and community from mere fame and visibility.

6

From Influence to Opportunity

British venture capitalist Harry Stebbings was 18 and faced the prospect of attending law school when he decided to become a VC. To learn everything about the art of being a venture capitalist, he started a podcast named The Twenty Minute VC to interview successful investors. He thought that by building relationships with VCs through the interviews, he could eventually get hired by one.

Without any contacts in the VC space, he spent £50 on a microphone and sent an email to Guy Kawasaki with an invite to interview him for a podcast. Kawasaki agreed, and Stebbings interviewed him from his family home's kitchen table. With a brand-name VC as his first reference, Stebbings took what he gained from that exposure to lure other well-known VCs to participate. The Twenty Minute VC podcast blew up and gained Harry a massive social media following. What's more, he learned everything about being a VC from the best, enabling him to kickstart his own fund at a young age.

Harry started by building social proof and affinity with the people he admired, helped them get positive recognition, and built an industry-wide network and professional reputation in the process. He is living proof of how influence can turn into opportunities.

Up to this point, we've been working on how you can become an influencer on social media. You started by setting goals to establish why you wanted to gather influence in the first place; then, you selected the best fit in terms of the social media platform, model, and audience–matching those with your intent.

Once online, you contributed to useful conversations and commented on the posts from others, all the while minding your responses to come across as empathetic, insightful, and just plain human. As people responded, you built your network. Now it's time to put your hard-earned following and influence to work to create opportunities.

Three considerations will guide your efforts. First, learning the differences between public and private conversations and how each can serve different purposes, expose your ideas to different audiences, and present yourself in different ways. Second, learning to use influence to create career opportunities for advancement, change, or other moves. And finally, learning to use your social media influence to grow your business or simply the organization you work for and care about.

Public vs. Private Conversations

It's undoubtedly common knowledge that public behavior differs from private behavior. That holds whether you're interacting IRL or virtually through social media. For example, to some extent, people interacting in a public online forum often feel freer to say bad things about others in the same conversation. They might draw conclusions about their character or intentions without really bothering to find out what lies beneath them. Or they might just be trolling, trying to juice up indignation or some other reaction for an ego boost or attention.

This kind of thing happens all too easily on social media and is more or less built into the system because of how we communicate there. Without the benefit of face-to-face interaction, where you might pick up on subtle tones or body language, you only have text to contend with, or at most, videos and images that are displaced from real-world context. You may misinterpret someone's post because of your filter bubble and be tempted to judge that person. You may accuse them of something or at the least assign meaning to them and their character based on your own cognitive biases rather than trying to understand what the person really meant.

To make such reactions even more complicated, there's often an unspoken assumption across online conversations that we don't expect people to be their authentic selves when they're in a public online forum in the same way as we expect them to be in a private online conversation. Some notable exceptions include private conversations that are scams like "catfishing" or someone pretending to be your friend asking for an emergency fund transfer. Beneath the flow of public online conversations we participate in, a vague, settled suspicion of pretense and a facade has become commonsense–it's baked into public social media interactions and taken for granted, oftentimes operating below our attention.

Public online conversations differ in many important respects from private online conversations, just as they do in real life. And while you need to participate in both, it's important to know the differences so you can make the best use of each forum. In private online conversations, the connection is more immediate and intimate. Communication challenges still exist, but you and your conversation partner are more likely to be more patient and forgiving to one another. If you have a question about what the other person meant in their remarks, you will probably ask for clarification before reaching a conclusion. The conversation and the relationship are important to you, the stakes are higher, and the interaction demands charity on both sides.

And while there are dramatic exceptions within a private conversation, such as scams, you're likely to set aside suspicion so that you can reach an authentic understanding with the other person. Ironically, using psychological triggers to alleviate suspicion and cynicism is a tool scam artists use to gain a victim's trust.

Even though both operate in a virtual environment, bonds within private conversations are stronger than in public conversations. Of course, if you're in an online conversation with someone you know in real life, that relationship will support the online one and ease the conversation. This can even happen within small online groups if the members have connections outside social media. Private WhatsApp groups for hobbies and the like are good examples.

The differences between public and private conversations drive the differences between outcomes you can expect and hope to achieve in either environment. Public conversations, especially among well-intentioned and genuine participants, are a place for building thought leadership because your insights, help, and introductions operate across a group. Thought leadership isn't much of an outcome if you're in a private conversation, even when the other person in the conversation endorses you and your ideas to others. Thought leadership in that context will remain at a different level than what's possible in public conversations.

Similarly, relationship building operates at different levels within public and private conversations. You can build relationships within public conversations, but the dynamics are such that you are building a relationship that operates at a "one-to-many" level rather than the "one-to-one" or "one-to-few" level of a private conversation. While your public relationships can bolster your credibility (and consequently your through leadership), they don't necessarily engender the deeper connection of private conversations or the level of trust those conversations can evoke.

One possible exception includes private interest groups. By definition, these groups are public, meaning more than two people join them. At the same time, the number of interlocutors is limited, and so the gap between public and private is narrowed, permitting relationship building that's in line with private conversations but taking place in a public forum. Think of any club or society of which you might be a member in real life–a similar dynamic operates in private interest groups.

Private interest groups are prey to confirmation bias and other kinds of in-group cognitive mistakes, so you should watch for those and how they might affect your interactions. To remain authentic and gain ground as a thought leader, it's best to find your ground to stand on, even within a private interest group. It's better if people respond to your posts and conversations at the level of idea and action rather than simply reacting to your membership in the group. Within any group, individual members have differences. How well a group can tolerate those differences is a subject we will address in Chapter 7.

Decide for yourself how large a group can be before you no longer consider it private. Social networks often establish guidelines about that, but they vary. But certainly, interactions in a 10,000-member "private group" are different than in a 100-member group. Another important fact about private groups is that they are controlled to one degree or another (as all online interactions are) by the social media network's algorithms. While AI might not be a direct influence, its power within the local social fabric surrounding the group and even outside the group contribute to individual behavior. Still, with those caveats, building relationships, influence, and thought leadership is possible in public groups, but they present in different ways.

Virtual Conversation Guidelines

With the differences I've laid out here, you might be wondering just what are the best tactics to use in public or private conversations when building influence. The main point: Behave in virtual groups, private or public, in ways that bring value to other group members and boost your recognition as a thought leader rather than simply drawing attention to yourself. The shortlist that follows covers the main points, and should help you stay on track, but it doesn't include all of the actions you can take in public and private situations.

What to Do and Not Do in Public Conversations

Do participate in public conversations initiated by relevant industry influencers. When you join conversations initiated by the people respected in the industry, you become affiliated with these people. That connection lifts your relevance within the industry simply because you are part of the conversation and their industry. This is especially useful because it doesn't require that you have any initial starting level–you can be a beginner with no experience whatsoever. You build your visibility when you contribute quality, timely comments to the right conversations.

Do start public conversations regularly in your area of expertise and engage in the conversations to keep them active. Once you are comfortable with starting conversations, you should. Open discussions about timely and relevant topics, and pull in industry influencers to create value for the whole community around you. When people in your industry look forward to your conversation openers, you have achieved a level of thought leadership. Once you start a conversation, be an active part of it. If you just share and abandon your posts, people will think of you as a content scheduler bot and disengage.

Do share positively about your encounters with relevant people. A key issue in public conversations is the building of affinity. WhenShare positively about that encounter when you meet someone in real life (at a conference, for example), share positively about that encounter. This way, you offer the stage to the person you met while creating a positive link between you. If you do this kind of sharing in public, it builds your status and professional brand, and it reinforces in people's minds your thought leadership and influence.

Do not try to sell your products and services in public wall conversations unless the poster specifically asks you to. Don't go on the public walls and try to sell stuff unless people ask for it. You see this kind of thing a lot, but those people will be seen as spammers by other industry people.

Do not send invites to potential clients with a cold sales pitch. The worst way to build your network is to send potential customers an invite that's actually a cold sales pitch. This isn't a good way to build a relationship, and it will make you look like a spammer. Conduct the lead-up to a sale in a private conversation after you've built some real-world trust with the person.

What to Do and Not Do in Private Conversations

Do join and participate in conversations in active industry groups. Seek active, discrete groups that are private enough to host high-quality conversations. Few public interest groups boast high-quality conversations, and you can consider them the equivalent of a public wall. Private interest groups are the best grounds for relationship building.

Do respond to publicly shared requests with private proposal messages. It's totally OK to approach someone in the group with information and services if they have asked for help with something, and you can offer a product that you think will assist them. Private messages ease the way into this process, and a private message will often carry more weight than overt commercial ones. Think of yourself as representing a solution to create this kind of "transaction plus" relationship.

Do talk about products and services in private conversations to build trust for future sales. Once you have built a relationship, you can continue to build trust by continued offers of help and advice. But remember–the relationship comes first. You need to give before you make an ask to avoid the other person dismissing you as a cold call or something. By giving first, you create in the other person's mind the characteristic of being a good person, mindful of more than business deals.

Do invite people personally to events you host. Inviting people you know in the social media space to events you're hoisting makes sense, and private conversations are powerful tools for that. Its power comes from the fact that a person can recognize a mutually beneficial opportunity in your exclusive private invitation. If they attend your webinar, for example, thank them for joining and think about asking for their thoughts on the session. In the best circumstance, the person who attends based on your invitation may respond with an invitation for you to attend their own event. These back-and-forth interactions are like rungs on a ladder that take you toward better industry relationships, greater visibility, and recognition as a thought leader.

Do not ask first because giving first builds trust. I've said it before, but it bears repeating: Don't ask for help or connection before giving something. For example, starting with "Can I pick your brain?", or "Would you have time for a meeting?" is asking something without giving something first. For example, you want to initiate a private conversation with somebody among your LinkedIn connections but not in your "close friends" circle. You believe this person is relevant to your own interests, so when they post on a particular subject, you comment on their post or send a private message to offer your help. In this way, you get the conversation going–and after a few interactions, establish the relationship between you; then, you can talk about your product and services in the context of their particular issue.

Do not try to sell your products and services through cold texts or instant message spam. Everybody gets a lot of text spam on different platforms. You know what it looks like: All you get is "Hello" and then a sales pitch. The chances someone you want to build a relationship with will respond to this tactic is very close to zero. Further, it reflects on your online character–you simply don't come across as an interesting partner by sending unsolicited messages to random people.

Advancing Your Career through Influence

If you're working just to earn money, you can stop reading this story now.

Aside from the undeniable financial burden, being unemployed is often perceived as not giving to others, not sharing your skills and knowledge, and not helping to make things a little better in the small world around you.

Michaela Alexis faced that truth in 2016. And she put it alongside something else she knew–the social media power of LinkedIn.

As she tells it, LinkedIn isn't a resume shop or the home to professional, humble bragging. It's really not a place at all but an endeavor. "If you're only using LinkedIn when you need it [to find a new job], it is like you would be selling an old couch on Craigslist," she writes, "you're doing it wrong."

Michaela had already spent years on LinkedIn polishing her profile, contributing to conversations, expressing her own perspectives, and connecting with a growing network of people. She traded advice, insights, milestones, invitations, and stories.

So it made sense to her to use all that effort as the backbone of her job search. She retooled all the usual job hunt approaches and doubled down on LinkedIn to land the marketing job she really wanted.

It took her two weeks to land her dream job, which the employer tailor-made for her.

To influence others in the interest of career building, you must be visible to them. Headhunters are more likely to find you, for instance, the more you are seen in the context of your expertise. Michael built visibility from nothing, and so can you. Unlike other periods when notice and influence were granted only from the recognition of legal and social entities. Today, your identity can be self-constructed and doesn't rely on outside power.

Greater Visibility Increases Remote Opportunities

Social media visibility brings further benefits in that it lets you create and practice influence from a distance. Remote work became familiar to many businesses during the COVID-19 pandemic when proximity fueled infection and disease. And while some companies have returned to demanding in-the-office work post-pandemic, many more are open to remotely hiring and supervising their workers. That means you can create a social proof of your skills, influence, and thought leadership without having to live in a large metropolitan area.

Much of what you need for more visibility and better opportunities you can create by being visible in social media discourse. With the right connections, which you have learned are built up from trusted relationships you establish in public and private venues and conversations, you increase your value as a remote employee or a freelancer. Endorsements from industry influencers go a long way to proving your worth in the job market. They make up the social proof that you're an engaged, thoughtful, and forward-leaning player in the industry conversations relevant to your professional and personal interests, regardless of your location or level of professional experience.

Every post you make is an opportunity to gain and leverage social proof. When people participate in your conversations, other people see who is commenting. By attracting influencers to the conversation on your own post, you gain an absolute endorsement as to who you are, what you're doing, and how valuable you and your efforts are. In the game of influence, targeting and pulling the right people (whom you've learned to identify and how to approach and connect with invites, introductions, and help) into the right conversations strengthens social proof and your capacity to be an influencer yourself.

As you achieve more visibility, it brings along with it the context that a headhunter or other hiring agent needs to make an initial assessment of your talents. And if hiring agents take an initial look into your background, they make a note of your participation and inevitably draw the conclusion that you're part of the conversation in the industry. You create a perception (which you should reinforce with your conversations) that you can be a trusted partner. Needless to say, if you're creating a phony identity just to build attention, you will soon be found out, and your online identity will take a big hit. That remains true whether you're trying to secure a position or if you want to advance in your career.

Grow Your Business with Influence

Three general tactics can be used to grow your business, whether you're an entrepreneur, marketer, salesperson, business developer, or have other business growth interests. The first is to grow inbound queries and interest, and sales by building an audience. The second is to improve conversions by building trust and providing social proof. The third is to turn your audience into a community.

Grow Inbound

When you think of building an audience, you're not likely to think of heat pump enthusiasts as a relevant audience. Just how on earth do you make people greatly interested in a necessary and mundane product like a heat pump? There are a lot of passions and interests to pursue on social media, but heat pumps?

Meet the "Heat Pump Man." Matti Perkkiö was the CMO of a Finnish heat pump company until the end of 2021. Matti branded himself the "Heat Pump Man" and became highly active on social media conversations related to his business.

Whenever there were social media conversations about heating systems, the Heat Pump Man was there to set things right. If you were talking about heat pumps, you were talking about the Heat Pump Man. He initiated what seemed like a never-ending series of new conversations about heat pumps. People, myself included, doubted that anyone could have the passion for talking about heat pumps for years. But new people always needed and found the Heat Pump Man, who was always available to talk about that essential home appliance. He was kind, caring, and helpful. The qualities you need to be a servant influencer. And a successful one at that.

Superpowers like those of the Heat Pump Man will get anybody's attention. As a result, Matti was instrumental in helping his company grow from 3M to 33M euros in revenue in a few years. Matti's company became the largest full-service heat pump installer in Finland by a large margin during his time as the Heat Pump Man. Having finished his mission, Matti retired from the Heat Pump Man and moved on to new challenges.

After leaving the heat pump company, Matti joined a software company in a rapid growth phase, heading toward its future IPO. He's now a marketing executive in an entirely new field that might be in need of its own superhero. But the legend persists. Everyone in Finland still remembers, and many still try to imitate, the legendary Heat Pump Man.

Improve Conversions with Social Proof

Every post you make is an opportunity to gain and leverage social proof. When customers talk about you, thought leaders participate in your post conversations, and the media contacts you due to your popular post, you are building social proof.

I wanted to kick start a community for my startup a few years ago. The challenge was to make it interesting to join the community early when there weren't any other members yet. I realized I needed social proof to get influential people to join.

This took the form of a single extremely well-planned and crafted LinkedIn post in which I made the pitch to join the community. The post didn't have any links to the signup page but simply asked to comment if they were interested in joining. I had pre-solicited a few influencer friends to comment on the post to remove the hesitation from others.

Every comment the post got also made the post visible to the networks of the commenters, with the commenter's "yes" creating a targeted social proof for their own networks. This led to the post going viral, and I ended up gaining 720 signups from that single post, a personal record.

What's more, I got to personally invite the people who commented into the community, warmly welcoming them to the community to which they were invited. With this tactic, I achieved two wins: Every person who commented on my post made it visible to their friends. The sharing created a situation in which others were exposed to my comment and connected to this early community I had alluded to. The number of comments on my feed began growing, and social proof emerged as everybody was already expecting to see many people they already knew. In essence, I built a community study from nothing. More than that, the community reached critical mass when I personally brought each commenter into the group.

As part of the onboarding process, I personally thanked each of them for playing a part and told them how excited I was that they had joined. Those private messages reinforced the personal trust that I was building with them. One process, two outcomes: Addressing a public conversation for social proof and a private conversation for personal relationships. It turned out to be one of the most successful campaigns I've ever carried out on social media.

The community ended up growing to 82,000 members from 182 counts over a short period of time.

Turn Your Audience into a Community

Leveraging your visibility can critically accelerate business growth, but staying visible in the daily feeds of your target audience is hard. Durable visibility forms the ground for a community—a stronger relationship than one built around business and target audience. Social media platforms and their algorithms constantly change, making it hard to predict if the audience you build will remain available later. Even if you build an audience on one platform, that platform might not remain popular.

For example, many companies built a large Facebook page following only to find out that Facebook changed their algorithms to reduce organic visibility almost to zero. As I mentioned in the previous chapter, a strategy I employed to move from audience to community was to post a request for people to comment if they were interested in an invitation to an exclusive early community.

So what are the advantages of a community over an audience? First, a community enables a direct line of communication with your fans with no intermediary filters. A community also interacts with your business in a way that spreads the word about your common cause because community members spread the word about your business on new platforms and other places to which you don't have access or reach. That mitigates the issue of an ever-changing social media landscape and a constantly fickle audience. You're able to engage people from different walks of life and enlist them in your cause. Tesla did this so successfully that it built one of the best-known brands in the world without spending a dime on paid advertising.

In the next chapter, we will examine what it takes to build a community. It all starts with turning your mission into a shared cause. The way there is to create a culture before you chase growth, and we'll be reminded that giving first is the only way to do that reliably. Finally, I will offer some guidelines to help hold your community together.

7

Building Communities

It was August 2017. I was building a startup in Berlin and experimented with LinkedIn algorithms with a group of growth hackers from all over the world. Using a slew of tactics, I gathered well over a million views monthly for my LinkedIn posts. It wasn't even that hard when the goal was simply to get views. For me, it was a way to learn about social media algorithms and how they work.

I realized that if I shared these insights with people who have good intentions, we could do a lot of good together. I came to the conclusion that the best way to do this was to build a community of influencers who commit to doing good with their influence.

I reached out to several Finnish influencers because I knew many of the most popular business influencers personally, and I thought it made sense to test the potential impact of a community inside a relatively homogenous demography. But even in a small country like Finland, there are factions. As an expat, I thought I could bring together a diverse group, at least in a local sense, without sparking too much infighting.

We started as an influencer peer support group sharing tips and tricks on expanding influence on social media, mainly on LinkedIn and Twitter. In the beginning, we tried to invite people with diverse backgrounds to be able to serve multiple bubbles effectively. In the early days, there were arguments and disagreements among the members, and as a result, some left. I saw it as the necessary process to find enough things that united us to be able to tolerate the things that divided us.

Once we had a critical mass and good enough diversity of members, we expanded the community rules to include impact goals. The idea was to help each other to build influence to make the world a little better place and to make the Finnish business social media scene a little more friendly and inviting to everyone.

We ended up promoting many important causes to the general public and collaborating in many different ways over the years. We have become close friends and still, today, wield considerable collective influence in Finland, with the group members collectively gaining millions of views monthly in a country of 5.6 million people and only a bit over a million monthly LinkedIn and Twitter users.

The group was originally built as a Facebook Group, but over the years, we expanded it to Telegram, WhatsApp, and Discord. WhatsApp eventually became our main communication channel, mostly because the notification deliverability leads to the best conversation experience. Today, after five years, I can proudly say that it is a community of true servant influencers that does make a positive difference.

Maybe you don't have a community right now. But if you've been following and practicing the ideas in this book, and you've given your work time to flourish and grow, then you should have a following.

If you're at that point, then you're ready to build a community. There isn't a hard and fast rule on when someone is ready to be a community leader. The number of followers you have isn't what's really important. Your capacity to influence and the fact that you have an audience you can move to are important starting points. You can measure the last, but you must first assess yourself. You will have to decide when your influence base will support community building. Here are some ideas for turning your audience into a community to help you focus on that decision and the next steps.

Why a Community?

Social media has become one of the main sources of growth for many different businesses and ideas. Under these circumstances, digital influence is the only influence that matters anymore because no other form of influence scales at the same efficiency and speed. It's a challenge that all companies face.

But a challenge arises from the very act of building audiences on social media. It's a fickle situation. When you build an audience, it persists so long as you're not "canceled" or are otherwise damaged in their eyes. On social media, many circumstances can destroy your fortunes in terms of your followers (your audience.) And when algorithms or circumstances change, your business must adapt quickly. The maintenance work to retain an audience becomes a long-term cost.

Building a community is a safer, more sustainable option. With a community in place, you have a direct line of communication with your clients, with no algorithmic filters. There aren't competing interests or hostile forces that can easily break a community – although it isn't impervious to all forces. In the end, a community offers a better way to communicate with customers.

Communities Are Not Audiences

Many businesses have a Facebook page, Instagram profile, or YouTube channel where they share ideas as the company itself. In some cases, the company's founders share ideas on social media as thought leaders. In either case, people react to those posts online, making up an audience.

The original message comes from a single or perhaps a handful of sources. The task of the followers is to watch and engage with the original content. The marketing team often handles this process to keep a steady stream of content flowing.

That's the dynamic of an audience. In a community, on the other hand, you will see many people sharing their own messages and sometimes the community leader's messages with other community members and with outsiders. When more people than your own employees share posts, you save on costs, and your messages reach far wider and deeper than possible if only your employees are sharing with your audience. The company's role is to support the community, be its champion, and align common interests, so that community members take the initiative to push things forward.

To build a community, you must think about how you will move from an audience-centric model into a community-centric model. Companies often confuse one with the other. They think that the audience is more or less a common name for a community, and they assign a "community manager" to curate the audience and be the person who shares posts on social media.

And there is where the notion of community falls apart for these companies. Because it's not a community they are interacting with, it's an audience. There's less organic visibility for your content because the people in the audience aren't sharing. People who join a community contribute broadly to keep the community going.

With a community, you can engage members who are passionate about the company's aims, products, or services. By targeting them, the company can connect with its "true fans." These community members are the foundation of a healthy community. Unlike an audience, which must be regularly refreshed, a community can become self-sustaining. True fans can support your cause much longer than your average employee does because, in the long run, your workers care more about their personal careers than the purpose your company serves.

Don't Make Transactions, Guide Journeys

Rapid changes and shifts in the social media environment demand businesses to rethink their value propositions to account for that natural dynamic. It's no longer sustainable to simply turn campaigns into transactions. A sustainable value can't be created that way in the current social media era. You need to develop customer journeys.

Start by sharing your journey and letting your community members share theirs for a full, end-to-end experience. A community plays an important part in sustaining your business that an ever-changing, vulnerable audience cannot. To build sustainable value, a community is necessary.

From Mission to a Shared Cause

Not only do companies often mistake their audience for their community, but they also wrongly think their audience cares about the company's mission. People don't commit to a cause that isn't their own. Just as you create a shared journey to enable a community to create value, so you must embrace a shared cause with your community. That's what makes people join and keeps people engaged with your community. Here's the winning formula:

Good Cause + Shared Values = Lasting Impact

You can build a community around any cause that other people share with you, provided that you can find these people and convince them to join. Only a mission driven by a good shared cause has a chance to grow into a great community. Your company's role is to support the cause, champion it, and let the members take their own initiative.

Ideal Community Members and What They Value

Who are your ideal community members? It's important to identify them because when you're building a community, you must build its culture–and culture can only be built on shared values. You can build a community around multiple sets of values. What's important is that your community members share those values with you.

When you set out the values for your community, define them, so they flex as the community evolves. That doesn't mean values are like chameleons, changing to suit the environment. It means that values take on new meanings and practices as the environment changes. Start with a few core values that unify community members, despite their individual differences.

For example, you may value a diverse community. That means that along with all the other identifiers people use to define themselves, you might also champion diverse perspectives, beliefs, and opinions. That basic value defines the self-selection community members adopt–if some potential community members don't accept the belief in and practice of diversity, it's hard for them to be part of that community.

The ideal community member is willing to share the experience of your shared journey with others. This dynamic is what makes the community tick. As multiple people share their experiences, the community becomes active and engaged. It grows stronger as members become willing to give before they ask. They sacrifice something for the cause before they look to gain something. When these are the qualities of your ideal community member, you have a strong foundation on which your community can grow.

Culture First, Growth Second

It's hard to build a strong culture. But you absolutely need to establish a community culture before you press for growth. Culture makes or breaks a community, and it depends on shared values to grow strong. You'll depend on the superfans within the community, those ideal community members, to carry the torch.

Superfans Spark Culture

Initiate your community culture build by enlisting superfans that you've hand-picked as fitting with everything that you're doing in terms of journeys, causes, and values. It's OK to build a small community. However, a small community of superactive fans is much better than a large collection of random people who don't have anything in common with each other or your goals. Communities gain value when they serve their members, and this value arises from superfans sharing and evangelizing.

Once a strong culture is established, people will want to belong to your community. If their values mesh with the community's, they will want to participate in the sharing and evangelizing pioneered by your superfans. As the culture takes shape and stabilizes, you can grow the community and retain that feeling among people that they want to be part of it.

Culture Sparks Subcultures

Some of the community's original members may not want to be part of a bigger forum. Or, they may have begun to form subcultures that carry even more value in their eyes than the main community. That's okay–people often gravitate toward niche groups that have more meaning. As part of community growth, remaining flexible in allowing the community to spawn subcultures will ease the pressure of the larger community's boundaries. Those who align with subcultures remain connected to the greater community's values as they enjoy the relational benefits–relational and emotional connections–they gain from the smaller ones.

Culture VIPs

Within any culture, as within any community, some members will be more active than others. Take care of your most active members–your cultural ambassadors–with VIP rooms and VIP treatment. Consider making them admins for the community's social network activity. The shared values at work among VIP members should align with the shared values of the entire community. That dynamic creates a strong level of intimacy, which you can foster to strengthen the community's culture. In fact, you often find that VIPs will take care of other members and bring them closer to the cultural center of the community, further bonding community members to shared values.

So let your VIPs play big roles in the community because they're going to act to unify members and further grow the culture so that it can grow. They will do it for a long time because they are loyal to the shared values among the community and between the community and your business. And as a benefit that far exceeds the value of maintaining an audience, VIPs will carry out this work for free because they care deeply about the community and its culture.

You may want to reward your VIPs beyond providing them their own space and with a recognized voice in the community. Don't pay them a wage. As soon as you start paying them regularly, they will see their role as a job. This will lose the cultural and social capital built into the VIP status. Give gifts if you like, or find other ways to recognize their contributions–but don't turn their passion into a job.

Keep Culture and Community Thriving

Community culture is organic and, in that sense, has a lifecycle like any other organic entity. However, there are several actions you can take to help your community thrive. Some important ones include establishing the community on the right platform from the start, notifications, and providing sensible, valuable incentives.

- **Notifications, Platforms, and Incentives**

Without notifications, fostering an engaged conversation with your community is impossible. And to set the stage for notifications, you have to pay close attention to which social media platform your current ideal community members use. For example, if you're targeting a specific niche, like NFT art enthusiasts, you can establish your community on Discord or Telegram. If you're working in a more traditional field, you will have to select a platform with generally older membership.

A big difference between chat platforms like Discord or Telegram and a wall-based community platform like Facebook groups is that the experience on chat platforms is more real-time. That actually makes a difference in relationship building. You feel like you know the person chatting with you in real-time more than you feel about someone who leaves a comment on your wall post 3 hours after you posted it. So the choice between wall threads and chat is a trade-off between staying current on things that interest you on your own time and building relationships while losing many potentially interesting conversations while you are away.

A challenge you face in selecting a platform best suited for your notifications is that they all have their own rules and limitations. WhatsApp, for example, has been the perfect app for notifications delivery. But part of why notifications worked particularly well for WhatsApp was that it had historically limited its maximum group size to 250 people, making sure every notification came from people you cared about.

From 2022 onwards, that changed, and WhatsApp started gradually increasing the maximum group size, which was at the beginning of 2023 at 1024 members. Time will tell if people joining larger groups will compel them to mute notifications, just like many have already done on Telegram.

The right incentives play an important role in a thriving community. You can't depend on altruism alone. Without suitable incentives for community members, you may end up with less activity and commitment than you want. So how do you come up with the right incentives? As you did with developing shared values, you must find a way to match community members' internal, individual desires with the external recognition and rewards they may receive for being active in the community. If you can incentivize acts of community members that promote altruistic causes, for example, you create an opportunity for virtue-signaling while scaling impact.

Give First–It's the Only Way

Communities aren't monoliths but collectives. They're composed of individual people. They're not a blended product of mixing people together. That's one reason building a community can be hard and building a culture even harder. In any community where people try to take from the group before giving to the group, the community will die. Frankly, if people don't share, they're an audience, not a community. And if people don't feel they gain more than what they give to the community, they will leave. The best communities support a culture (and draw support from a culture) that gets people to give first. It won't last long if your community doesn't have a give-first culture.

To give first means "to offer thoughts, insights, advice, introductions, or help without expecting an instant return." Giving first promotes reciprocity. You don't worry about your gain because you have built relationships and social capital that adds more value than what you gave.

Sustainable communities create value that exceeds each individual's contribution. If you end up in a situation where most of the people are just there to take from a small group of givers, the givers will eventually burn out and lose interest. One by one, they will bail out until, eventually, nobody's giving. On the other hand, a positive giver-taker ratio creates a huge multiplier that also amplifies your organization's value.

You will have to work to retain a level of balance where there's always more value available than what a community member can gain on their own. I often see companies building groups (with the idea of creating a community) where the only person sharing anything is the company's community manager. That's not a community–it's an audience.

While it's a lot of work to maintain the giver-taker equilibrium, it's still more efficient than maintaining an audience. So keep an eye on the balance, intercede when you have to (VIP members will likely do this work without prodding), and the cultural momentum takes on a life of its own–it's easier to keep balance as time goes on.

Guidelines to Keep It Together

Every community should have clearly set rules for its members. These rules and guidelines, when enforced properly, create a safe space for the members to communicate with each other. In creating those guidelines, it's important that you include a statement of the values so that members understand what they have in common among themselves and with you.

You may need to update the guidelines as your community grows. For example, if the community outgrows its original mission, early members may feel disconnected and leave the community—or if they care about the cause deeply, they may begin to challenge the new reality. You have to be mindful of this and enable the community to have subcultures and smaller groups to facilitate a reasonable diversity of ideas.

Community rules have to implement the community's values, giving members an incentive to subscribe to them when joining. Along with rules, encourage users to behave in ways that make the community safer and better. Ask members to help each other. Let the members see the community as a common cause, not just a group. Rules combined with recommendations will make your community a safe, trusted, and caring space for its members.

In addition to encouraging positive behavior, you should discourage negative behavior. No matter how open you want your community to be, you can't tolerate behavior that goes against the community's values. If someone is trolling the group or engaging in other activities that are not aligned with the community's values, remove them quickly. If you let people like this hang around, other people–the people you want to keep in the community–will leave.

Quick removal of people who create trouble in the community suggests and reinforces for other members that the rules do matter– not because it's a means of control but because it's a means of creating a safe space for everyone to participate. I've done this myself many times, and every time the atmosphere in the community has improved due to the removal of the troublemaker.

Winning Algorithm for Communities

Recruit Influencers to Reach Relevant Audiences

If you are building a diverse community, one of the main challenges is how to reach and convince members of different filter bubbles to join. In the community's early days, there's always a risk that the early members represent a niche demographic that makes people with different backgrounds shy away from joining.

You can mitigate this risk by carefully selecting influential early members who represent diverse backgrounds, enabling you to appeal across filter bubbles and cultural and demographic boundaries.

Build an Empathetic Culture that Cuts off Haters

An empathic culture cuts out haters. If people are empathetic toward each other, they will quickly organize to force the haters out. An added benefit is that community action helps you save time from moderation. Further, an empathetic atmosphere makes community members feel validated that they are in the right place.

Use Notification Flows to Keep People Engaged

People are bombarded with information while online. Leading social media platforms have conditioned everyone to expect instant responses when sharing something. If your community members don't get responses to their messages in a timely manner, they feel demotivated to share.

To enable a healthy and timely conversation between community members, you have to master the notification game. Without notifications, you can't have trust-building real-time conversations, just comments on posts over a longer period of time.

Subcommunities Maintain Intimacy–So Let Them

As I wrote earlier in this chapter, enable your community to split into smaller subgroups when it grows bigger. This way, people can retain intimacy and trust with their close circles while staying connected to the larger community. The main community and subcommunities combine to strengthen the entire community over time. WhatsApp understood this and launched a new service Whatsapp Communities, that enables you to have a main channel with many smaller subgroups under a community umbrella.

In the next chapter, we will move from communities to the project of making a lasting, positive impact. From making friends to building influence to creating a community where you can practice that influence–that's the path toward positive change.

8

Make a Positive Impact that Lasts

I described my own journey toward this idea in the Preface that opens this book. At a point in my life, I realized that I had to change in positive ways to help others so that they would help even more people and together make a change that benefits all.

The changes I made included breaking the bubbles, or silos, in my mind so that I could see people and situations as they were, not as I imagined them. My growing emotional intelligence supported me as I developed a greater capacity for empathy, and I was able to put myself in others' situations. From that perspective, I could see myself and imagine others as being on a journey to become "servant leaders," a phrase coined by Robert Greenleaf in his seminal 1970 essay, "The Leader as Servant."

As you might have guessed already, the title of this book, The Servant Influencer, arises from the concept of servant leadership applied to influencing.

Be the Change You Want To See in the World

While this phrase strikes many as a grand and improbable goal, it's not. The key is not to read it as changing the world, but as becoming, in yourself, the human being you think would inhabit the world you want to live in. We all have different ideas about what that world would look like and how it would operate. Assuming your view of the world doesn't consist of global domination with you at the top, the world you imagine is probably one in which all creatures thrive (including humans) and enables prosperity for all: peace, good health, and economic stability. And all you need to do, this phrase says, is to act as though that is the world you live in and behave and think accordingly.

This book proposes a path toward positive digital influence. If you're fortunate enough to become an influencer, remember: Digital influence is a superpower that must be used carefully. To wield it responsibly so that you are helping create a world with prosperity for all, keep these three keys in mind:

- Have a healthy purpose.
- Advocate healthy behavior and goals.
- Do not manipulate people to behave against their own good.

Healthy Purpose

To influence toward a healthy purpose, focus on how you can help others. Some people refer to the familiar *golden rule* from the Bible: "Do unto others as you would have them do unto you." Others point out the fallacy embedded in that construct: believing everyone else is just like you. Tony Alessandra and Michael O'Connor suggest *the platinum rule*: "Treat others the way they want to be treated."

Use that piece of emotional intelligence to help you think about how your existence can leave the world a better place. Follow the ancient code of ethics from about 400 BCE attributed to Hippocrates, a Greek physician, which is today a part of the Hippocratic Oath: "First, do no harm."

Machiavelli might dismiss such thinking as idealism that has no power or sustainability in the real world. But we don't live in 16th Century Italy. We live in a globalized, always-on, ostensibly transparent, and boundary-less world brought about by technology and one of its most far-reaching products: social media.

To sustain your healthy purpose, work on things that give you joy. Not everyone has the privilege of finding joy in their work. For some, work is a matter of survival. If that's where you are, it's still possible to find activities that will bring you joy. When learning to play a musical instrument, for example, you will have to work at it consistently for a period of time. But along the way, even the frustration of learning and failing will lead to glimpses of joy. You can also take a completely different path and host small, intimate dinners for neighbors and friends. Look for the joy in the connections that unite us.

Advocate Healthy Behavior and Goals

In the realm of social media and in the more immediate world of real-world social relations, try to be a force for good by not glorifying extremes. People don't react well to extremes. When they are confronted with an extreme position or argument, or treatment, they tend to respond emotionally. That's just how humans are wired–fight or flight–to behave in confrontations. And that's why social media sometimes feels so toxic. Always try to add balance.

That doesn't mean you can't find passion in your beliefs or find errors in the reasoning and reactions of others. Just find a way to express and act on your passions in ways that don't spark a confrontation. There's nothing wrong with our emotions–they are embedded in us. But the rapidly acted emotional response to a confrontation can overwhelm rationality, the mode of thinking that allows us to take a different perspective, think bigger, and seek to understand. Unite your fast and slow thinking into a balanced assessment of situations and others.

Human interactions balanced between confrontation and reason form the basis of a working world. Some communities–faith-based, political, and others–seek that balance, learn to accept the messiness of differences common to our social lives, and strive to prosper amid the muddle. It's no different on social media. Your commitment to balance can strengthen your influence as it makes room for others to speak their minds.

To influence effectively, you must meet people where they are. Realize that your ideas don't suit everyone. You can't escape the necessity of a point of view. But keep in mind, as Bertrand Russell wrote, "there is no reason to suppose that only one coherent body of beliefs is possible."

The fact that ideas, beliefs, and knowledge are different between one person and another isn't a call for confrontation. It's a call for learning and for practicing emotional intelligence. You may want to influence someone toward a belief that you think is more beneficial, but before you can start, you have to recognize the difference between their beliefs and yours and that we are all entitled to have beliefs about the world.

Don't Manipulate People to Act against Their Own Good

The world has no shortage of despots and scoundrels seeking to manipulate others for personal benefit. But the tools of their manipulation are not based on influence. They are based on violence, surveillance, and threats to personal security. That is the world that needs changing. If you want to help make the world a better place for us all, then steer your influence away from selfish manipulation.

Some influences, like scams and trolling, are hurtful and dangerous. Unfortunately, money, power, and fame often flow toward parties who are manipulating facts, impersonating trusted sources or otherwise harmfully shaping beliefs to benefit themselves. The success of criminals and wrongdoers is always temporary but can have devastating effects on individual lives as it happens. Influence cannot escape motive–so adopt a positive motive when wielding your influence superpower.

One peculiar and particularly harmful manifestation of social media is the rise of cancel mobs. People can be robbed of their peace of mind, threatened by strangers, and lose their livelihoods because of mob attacks on social media. Too often, these mobs form in the court of rumors and opinions and end up destroying innocent lives. It never benefits you to take part in a cancel mob. The smug satisfaction you might get from judging and publicizing someone else's behavior is nothing more than an incentive for manipulators to engage you in the service of their often nefarious goals if you are insulted, by all means, object. But do it first personally, and don't channel your rage through a mob that is indifferent to the ethics of human-to-human connection.

You can't make a better world by creating false consciousness. Honest appraisal, acceptance of different perspectives, and transparent influence toward sustainable benefits is the only path open to you.

Break Bubbles to Open Your Mind

I made an observation early in this book that we are all in some kind of bubble. Whether it's self-imposed or based on algorithms, your bubble colors your beliefs, behavior, perspectives, and other aspects of your life. Sometimes we call these bubbles silos or comfort zones. The algorithms at work in social media reinforce the bubbles we are in. But bubbles aren't inescapable prisons, and they aren't all-powerful or all-encompassing. By consciously making that choice, you can break out of your bubble and learn to think more openly and generously.

Similarly, your online character is a product of the bubbles you hang out in. Confirmation bias affirms your beliefs within the bubble and works against contrary voices. Algorithms work to keep you in your bubble and reinforce the benefits (although incomplete) that come from belonging to the group.

Understand the same applies to everyone. If you are confronted online or you begin a new online connection, the person you're communicating with has a worldview shaped by their experience. They spend time in their comfort zone. Algorithms help in keeping them there. Be generous and patient in your interactions. We have different experiences, different cultures, and different beliefs–but there is commonality amid the differences.

Build Trust with People Outside Your Bubble

You start as a non-partisan to build trust. Your motive should be to create a relationship and the trust that supports it. That doesn't mean that you have to give up your firmly held beliefs. But if you carry your worldview into every interaction like a flag, and you use that flag to beat people over the head–those outside your bubble won't trust you.

There's a way to hang out with people outside your bubble. Join a couple of interest-based groups with people from other bubbles to learn how they think. Find the things you have in common with people in other bubbles and use them in your communication to build trust. Start there, not as an adversary but as an empathetic conversationalist, and offer help where you can.

Communicate in Their Language

People in different bubbles, like people in different cultures, speak differently and may use different language than you do to communicate with others in their group. You must know this from life experience–do you know people who use a dialect of the home language you share that you aren't familiar with? Do you make judgments based on that?

Learn and join their conversation using the language they use to build trust. Be careful, though–you want to use the language correctly, or you may come off as hostile, making fun of others. Communication isn't based on language as much as it results from negotiation toward a common sense of things.

To communicate effectively with people different from you, draw on your empathy to let them know you understand their side of the story. Or if you don't understand, let them know that you accept that some people have different viewpoints from yours and that we are all entitled to our views. Truth too often seems a rarity. But there are things you don't know and things they don't know that are shaping what you believe is true. In many circumstances, chasing a singular truth isn't as important as the conversation itself.

Find a constructive way to make arguments. Empathy can help you read the emotion "in the room" and understand why others react to you the way they do (the core of emotional intelligence). If it's something in your behavior, make a change. Logic can help you establish the whys of your beliefs and understand why others might believe differently. Emotion is almost always stronger than reason when it comes to argument, but it too often summons reactions that are hard to control. Argue succinctly, and empathize emotionally. Your online character–how you are perceived (credible, angry, snobbish) accompanies you into every online interaction. So pay attention to how you appear to others.

Put Yourself in Other People's Position

Your worldview is the product of your upbringing, your life experiences, and the society you live in. In the real world, your worldview gives you a certain perspective of the world. It encourages you to take on some beliefs and avoid others.

As I said earlier, we have more in common than we have differences. That's where you want to put your focus. So where can you look to find the things that unite you?

Sometimes, it's family values. Treasuring your family is nearly a universal trait, even though, in practice, it looks different among different cultures, different generations, and even among individuals within a single family. Compare how you value family with those that express that value differently from you.

Other times, it's work that is common to you. All honest work has dignity. There isn't "work" and then "real work." Those are beliefs rooted in experience, a lack of information, or some other source–like class or prejudice. Whether you're a junior scientist working in a lab or a manual laborer repairing a road under a blazing sun, both of those jobs can be difficult and tiring in their own way. But both are productive and, hopefully, make the world a little better. Both are valuable contributions to society. Honor that in others.

Still, other times, you might share a cause or a hobby. Or you might have had experience in the same country. You may share a religion. You might even share frustration and distaste for how the political leaders in your country perform. It sounds paradoxical, but at some level (and it's a level you have to work with the other person to find), within every difference, there is commonality.

Be a Servant Influencer

Take on the mantle of a servant leader to become a servant influencer. From there, you can hope to be the change you want to see in the world. Mahatma Gandhi said it well: "If we could change ourselves, the tendencies in the world would also change. As a man changes his own nature, so does the world's attitude towards him."

A servant leader works to assist and develop others so they can reach their potential and pass on the lessons they learn. In the same way, a servant influencer will help and educate people. In earlier chapters, I wrote about helping others as an early stage in building online influence. That and similar work are the steps into servant influence.

Enable others to share your cause. Many people want to be part of something bigger than themselves. As you've worked through this book, you have probably formed an idea of a cause you want to pursue. It could be professional, such as creating a community that will lift your business into greater success, or maybe it's a passion that you want to make room for in your life. Extend a welcome to others to take part in your journey and help them to make your cause their cause.

Along the way, celebrate the success of others. Your personal goals are important to you, but others have their own. Help them reach those goals and then honor their progress. Let them learn as you learn, and be a guide for their efforts.

As your network expands and your influence grows, you will likely find real purpose and meaning in your work, whether in the creative field or on the business side of things. We often read that we should do what we love, but few people have that luxury. As a servant leader concerned more with the growth of others than yourself, joy comes from the help you give. So give generously, and reap the reward.

9

A Purposeful Life

As I grow older, my priorities continue to change. Instead of running from one superficial conversation to another at cocktail parties and networking events, I tend to look for one or two people who interest me and engage them in long, deep conversations about life, the universe, and the meaning of it all. These conversations are incredibly rewarding.

One of my favorite topics in such discussions is the popular philosophy that you should live every day as if it were your last day. But I put a twist on it: I live every day like it was my first day.

The main takeaway from this philosophy is to remain open to learning new things. With every decision we make, we need to decide if we want to explore something new or exploit our existing knowledge. We need to decide whether we want to step forward into growth or back into safety.

I have definitely taken my share of steps into uncertainty. I have often blindly trusted my good luck and hoped for good things to come; sometimes, the luck hasn't been as good as I'd hoped. Sometimes things have gone exceedingly well. The most important learning in all this is that I have learned to remain humble in the face of challenges. I strive to keep the beginner's mind.

I've built many new memories (and new synapses, no doubt) by living in multiple countries, studying new subjects, avoiding developing routines, and not planning my vacations in advance. I developed a child-like excitement about my passions and startup ideas, and I've tried hard to hang on to that.

Living many of my days like it was a new day of new life has been liberating. I'm deeply grateful that I figured that out early. I prefer to stay hungry and foolish.

I have joked to my friends that I have already contributed to bringing kids into the world and continued the circle of life, so the universe has no other purpose for me. By accepting my life as a meaninglessly tiny piece of the universe, I can be at peace with my mortality. I can also be at peace with the fact that no matter what I accomplish during my lifetime, it won't make much of a dent in the universe.

But I'm ok with that. Trying to make that small dent - like Apple's famous founder Steve Jobs did - still gives me purpose. Every time I succeed in helping a fellow human to learn a new thing or create a memory, I gain happiness and meaning.

Using influence to serve people is deeply meaningful and a fulfilling way to spend the social capital earned from the activities of an entrepreneur.

www.ingramcontent.com/pod-product-compliance
Lightning Source LLC
Chambersburg PA
CBHW071405210526
45465CB00001B/256